GO AROUND THE WORLD AND TELL MY CHILDREN I LOVE THEM

To Jenny ~

God bless you!

Esther B

Sharon Dryor

GO AROUND THE WORLD AND TELL MY CHILDREN I LOVE THEM

One woman's quest to hear and obey God's voice

ESTHER BENNETT with SHARON PRYOR

CONTENTS

By faith Abraham, when called to go to a place he would later receive as his inheritance, obeyed and went, even though he did not know where he was going.

—Hebrews 11:8 (NIV)

INTRODUCTION

I CAN'T REMEMBER A time when the plaque wasn't there. It was made out of glass with silver lettering and had scallops around the edges. The plaque was large—maybe fifteen inches long and three inches high. It hung over the archway that went into the front room. Every move we took—Rainier, Alberta, to Calgary, Alberta, to Riderwood, Washington, and finally to Sweet Home, Oregon—the plaque was always in that same place. It was just a part of the furnishings, so I never really saw it.

One day, in my fourteenth year, I was walking from the front room into the kitchen in our Sweet Home house when it dawned on me what it actually said: "JESUS SAVES." I realized that it had been there all along, and I hadn't really seen it until that moment. It was the same story that I had been learning at Bible camp: "Jesus is my Savior." The message had been there for years, and I hadn't even noticed it. Even though we never talked much about religion, the plaque was a silent witness in my house that we were Christians. I understood that my dad taught me by example, not by words, that we were a family whom Jesus died for.

I was challenged at Bible camp that if I read my Bible every day, God would change me, and others would recognize it—I wouldn't even have to tell them. That was a real test for me, so I decided to take up that challenge by reading my Bible each morning.

As my high school graduation approached, I asked God what I should do with my life. College? A career? A favorite teacher took me aside and said, "Esther, don't waste your life. Don't miss this opportunity to get an education; you will regret it." Still, I didn't know what to do. That morning, just weeks before graduation, God spoke through His word in Proverbs 16:16 (NIV): "How much better is it to get wisdom than gold, to get insight rather than silver." I interpreted that to mean I should go on to school. I went in to my dad and announced, "I'm going to college."

"All right," he said, "that's good." I would be the only one of his kids to get a degree.

Those experiences of hearing God's voice through written words laid a foundation in my life that He used to build on with His whispers in my heart. This book tells some of those stories. In these pages, you will see pieces of my spiritual life. You'll read about my first world trip, portions of over twenty trips to Southeast Asia, and my first time in Africa, plus stories from three of our Israel trips. These stories are a mosaic. Some names have been changed to protect privacy. My prayer is that the Holy Spirit uses these memories to help you to know Him better. I would encourage you to pray right now: "Jesus, if You are real, become real to me."

Even though it is common practice not to capitalize pronouns that refer to God, I have chosen to do it to honor Him. Most scripture quotes are from the King James Version (KJV), as that is what I carried with me on my first world trip. Others are as shown.

Many stories are still to be told—yours and mine—as we listen to His voice and follow the directions of our God.

Esther Bennett
Meridian, Idaho
November 2016

PART 1
MY FIRST WORLD TRIP

1

LEARNING TO LISTEN AND OBEY

GREEN BEANS AND CREAM

My heart was yearning for more of God. I read the scriptures often, taught Bible classes, hosted home groups in my house, and kept busy for God, but something was missing. I was like a lot of other people who go to church—bored and not at all excited about my spiritual walk. I prayed, though admittedly with little faith. I knew I was far from where I wanted to be.

One day, after I'd become increasingly aware of this unsettling feeling, David, one of my former students, dropped by my house. He asked my opinion about where he should go to college. High school graduation was fast approaching, and the pressure was on to know what to do with his future. As we chatted, I heard myself say, "Dave, have you ever heard God's voice?"

"I don't think so," was his reply. I heard a little voice within me say, *Have you?* I wondered why I had asked that question; now it was directed back to me!

I promised him I'd be praying about his future, and after Dave left, I made a trip to my bedroom, now my confessional. On bended knee, I asked Jesus to speak to me. I waited for what seemed like a long time. Nothing. I didn't hear a word. Then my reasoning and

Satan's attack took over. I heard a voice, but it wasn't pleasant. The voice said, "You know God speaks through His Word. Isn't that enough?" I got up off my knees, but I felt disappointed. I had hoped God would say something personal. Surely the One who made ears and mouths could speak to His child.

A week passed, and another weekend rolled around. Nothing happened out of the ordinary, so I decided to do my weekly grocery shopping. As I pushed my cart around the Albertson's store, a thought came strongly to my mind. *Buy green beans.* That idea grabbed my attention. Green beans weren't on my list. *I don't want green beans*, I told myself, yet the thought persisted. Even as I stood in the long Saturday-morning checkout line, it returned: *Go back and buy green beans.* I stood my ground even as I made it to the cashier and somewhat hesitantly paid for my groceries. Why was that impression so strong?

When I got home, I checked my cupboards out of curiosity. No green beans anywhere, even in the freezer. *Oh well*, I reasoned. The store was only blocks away—I could get some anytime.

As I continued to put my groceries away, the front doorbell rang. There was a Bible study friend with her four-year-old son. We hugged, and she asked if I had some time, as she needed to share some things. Soon we found ourselves deep in conversation that continued until her son demanded some attention.

I looked at my watch, realizing it was lunchtime, so I asked Jean if she would like to stay for lunch. I had leftovers in the refrigerator; all I had to do was add a vegetable as a side dish, and everything would be ready. I called Jean from the kitchen and asked what vegetable her son would like. Her reply sent shock waves through my whole body. "He's a funny kid." She laughed. "He only likes green beans."

I don't recall anything else that happened after that comment except that when Jean left, I headed back to my bedroom. Down on my knees, I told God I didn't know that was His voice I heard in the grocery store. "I didn't know You would talk to me about green beans," I apologized. I was sorry, but would He please try me again? I'd be listening next time.

The Monday morning after my green bean incident, I was getting ready to leave for work when I heard that Voice. *Take cream for your coffee*, it said. I stopped with my hand on the door. Once again I reasoned with the Voice. "I don't drink cream in my coffee," I replied. My friend Pat was the only one who came to my room, and she didn't drink coffee at all. In fact, she didn't even drink tea; all I'd ever seen her drink was water. What to do?

I grabbed my lunch and drove off to school. Now I was hearing things. *Esther, get a hold of yourself*, I scolded.

As Pat came by my room, she asked how my weekend went. Pat and I taught in portable classrooms that were used for overflow classes and were separate from the rest of the school. We seldom went into the actual school building and became quite good friends. I'd been talking with her about spiritual things because she didn't know the Lord at all. I responded, "Great! God spoke to me about green beans!" That grabbed Pat's attention.

"Tell me more," she urged and came into my classroom while I set up my art display.

As I related God's grace and kindness to a four-year-old boy and his mom, I told Pat He surely cared for her as well. She listened to my green bean story with great interest and then said, "I never drink coffee, but if you have some cream, I'll have a cup with you."

My heart sank. "Oh no, Pat! Father told me to bring cream for your coffee, and I rationalized that voice away and disobeyed Him. I didn't bring any cream. Please forgive me," I asked. Tears were close to the surface as I realized that I had messed up again.

"Did God really tell you to bring cream for my coffee?"

"Yes, Pat, and because I tried to reason instead of trusting, you didn't get your cream."

Pat was so moved by this that she went to her classroom and gratefully sobbed her way into God's kingdom. I marveled at His timing; Pat's first hour was her prep time, and she was able to calm down a bit before her second-hour typing class. Her life would be forever changed; many years later, she even took a mission trip with me to Thailand.

As I returned to my home at the end of the day and once again asked for forgiveness, I admitted I wasn't doing very well at listening. I asked again for another chance to hear His voice. As an athlete, I was hoping for three strikes before I was out. I already was down two strikes, but I told Him I'd try harder.

The next day was Sunday. Surely I'd hear God's voice at church. I turned my spiritual hearing aids up to high, but not a word. I was really trying to hear the Lord's voice; it was exciting to think about God speaking, but I wasn't hearing a single thing.

It was another Saturday morning, and I was busy cleaning house. Suddenly, over the roar of the vacuum cleaner, I heard that Voice again. *Go next door, and tell Macy I love her.* I shut off the vacuum, sat down on the couch, and once again tried to reason with the Voice.

"Now, Lord," I said, "You know I've tried to approach Macy on different spiritual subjects, and all my efforts have failed. Please give me something else to do." To me, Macy's spiritual life seemed nonexistent.

You promised you would obey whatever I asked.

"But, Lord," I countered, "how can I do this?" At my refusal, His presence literally moved out of my living room, and instantly my house felt like I'd turned on the air conditioning in December.

Before I knew it, I felt my legs taking me out of my door and across my driveway. The cold emptiness I experienced when His presence left my house was more than I could take. My finger pressed Macy's doorbell. Trembling, I waited. Now a clear voice jeered, "What are you going to *say?*" I recognized that voice, but it wasn't heavenly. I had no idea what I would say. I was relieved when Macy came to the door and greeted me warmly.

"Won't you come in?" she said.

We walked into her living room, and then she disappeared into the kitchen to put on the coffeepot. I began to calm down. Then I heard the gentler green bean Voice.

See, that wasn't so hard, was it?

As Macy brought two steaming cups of coffee in and sat down across from me, I said, "Macy, are you wondering why I came over?" She smiled in response, so I continued. "As I was vacuuming my front room, I heard the Lord say, 'Go over to Macy's house, and tell her I love her.'"

She teared up immediately. "I've wondered many times if He really does love me," she said. She went on to say that all six of her kids were out and her husband was called in to work, and that was why her home was so quiet that morning. It wasn't hard to see how Father had set the stage for Macy's special day. Then, in His wonderful way, He let me introduce Macy to her King. As I went home rejoicing, I had no idea what lay ahead, but Father knew.

Days passed, and I continued to try to obey all the directions I heard. I was learning that God only works for our good, and He needs obedient servants. He teaches us to obey His still, small voice. Greater things were ahead.

Several weeks later, I learned there had been a terrible accident that involved some woman who was returning from dropping her children off at school. Apparently, the brakes failed, and her car surged on to a main highway, where she was hit by a large truck. Her body was thrown out of the car and dragged by the truck. Much of her hair and part of her ear had been scraped off her head. I didn't know until later that day that it was my friend Macy who was in the accident and that she wasn't expected to live.

I poured out my heart to the Lord. "Dear Jesus," I prayed, "Macy has six kids. Please spare her life." I felt led to call friends and church folks for more prayer. What else could I do? Two things came to mind: make dinner for Len and the kids and keep praying.

After Len returned home from the hospital, I hurried over to see him. He was still sitting in his car with his face down on the steering wheel as he sobbed. I tapped on his car window, and as he raised his head, I saw a face filled with grief, fear, and bewilderment. He rolled down the window, and we talked as I assured him of many people's prayers and our willingness to help. He gratefully received the meal I'd prepared but told me he didn't know of anyone praying for him. As we cried together, I again assured Len that Jesus knew and was with his dear Macy that moment.

Walking back across our driveways, I was so grateful for a loving Lord who once again had gone before us to prepare the way of salvation and healing. Macy's recovery was long and slow, but Jesus was with her through it all.

And your ears shall hear a word behind you, saying,
"This is the way, walk in it,"
when you turn to the right or when you turn to the left.

—Isaiah 30:21 NASB

May your unfailing love be my comfort, according to
your promise to your servant.

—Psalm 119:76 (NIV)

God is our refuge and strength, an ever-present help
in trouble.

—Psalm 46:1 (NIV)

2

NINTH-GRADE GRADUATION

I T WAS EARLY June of 1972, and my junior high students were graduating. They were excited, chattering, and noisy; school was almost over, and summer lay ahead. Schoolwork was all done, and the students could almost taste their freedom.

I wasn't nearly as excited as I prepared to get changed for the evening ceremonies. I grumbled to myself about what to wear and said out loud, "When do *I* get to graduate? I've attended nineteen junior high graduations. I wish *I* could graduate."

Suddenly, a Voice said clearly, *Whenever you're ready.* I stopped there in the hallway, stunned by that impression. I lived alone, so it wasn't a human voice that had responded to my complaints. Did God say that? It was unmistakable, so clear. Did He say I could graduate whenever I was ready? That thought held me—challenged me—and made me wonder what I would do if I did indeed graduate.

I realized how tired I was. I was tired of grading long papers, reading reports, and working with crazy teenagers. At forty, I felt old and weary.

With graduation nearly over, I could still hear that Voice rolling around in my head like a tape recorder on replay. Again, I wondered, what *would* I do? I'd been a public schoolteacher for nineteen years and had made it to the top of the pay scale. My skills reflected the areas of my training—six years of higher education in athletics, health, geography, history, art—not worth much for anything except teaching junior high. Wearily, I crawled into bed and prayed for God to lead me if I was to make a lifework change.

It was a few days after that when I clearly awoke from a deep sleep. The alarm clock by my bed said it was 3:00 a.m. My room was dark and quiet, and a sweet presence seemed to fill my bedroom. Peace was everywhere—absolute calm and a deep quietness. All of a sudden, I was wide awake, so I sat up and said, "Is that You, Jesus?"

He answered, *Yes.*

I was not used to spiritual encounters in the night. I said, "What do You want?"

He replied, *I want you to go around the world and tell My children that I love them.*

He didn't use the word "missionaries," but I knew that was who He was referring to when He said "children." "Don't they know that?" was my irreverent answer.

Yes, they do, but they need to be reminded.

I was stunned. When I went to bed earlier that night, I had no inkling that I would have a holy visitation.

"Who will go with me?" I had toured Europe with a teacher friend but had never considered going on a long trip by myself.

I will, came the answer.

My limited intimacy with my personal God was hardly adequate for such a trip. I followed with the selfishness that was in my heart. "What will I get out of this?" I asked Him. The answer came in heavenly music as I sat there in His cool, beautiful presence. I heard,

"Through it all, through it all, you'll learn to trust in Jesus, you'll learn to trust in God."[1]

My eyes gushed with tears as my entire bedroom filled with angels' voices singing. Their song came through the floor, the ceiling, and all four walls, voices beyond any I'd ever heard. I was lost in wonder and love and aware that God would be the presence I would have to keep me company on my not-too-distant journey around the world. I would go and remind His missionaries that He loved them. I would learn that it was a message that was desperately needed.

---

1 "Through It All," by Andrae Crouch. © 1966, renewed 1994, by Manna Music Inc. (ASCAP).

3

MY PRINCIPAL

THE NEXT MORNING, I headed out to school. I had made the decision to tell my principal my exciting, life-changing news. He was a churchgoing man, a nice Lutheran. I was sure he would share my enthusiasm.

He was in his office, and I had to pass his door on my way to the mailboxes. Filled with excitement for my new call, I stuck my head in and said, "Hi, are you busy?"

"Not too busy—what do you need?"

I told Mr. Willis casually that I was going to quit my job and go around the world to tell God's people He loved them.

"Shock" is not adequate to describe my friend's response. He began to fidget, moving papers on his desk as he tried to find something to say. It finally dawned on me that my request must have really been a bomb. This poor man had no idea how I had come to this conclusion. I tried to back up a bit and explain. Clearly, I had frustrated and alarmed him.

He finally found the words he was searching for. "Maybe you need a sabbatical!" I was just tired, he suggested, and probably needed a rest. How else could he explain such a rash move by this stable career teacher he'd worked with for years? He said, "I just saw this paper telling faculty members that if they had any requests for the next year, they need to apply at the central office before the end of the day." He further suggested maybe I should go and apply for a sabbatical for the coming year. If it was accepted by the school board and funded by an upcoming tax-levy vote, that would give me the money I needed to pay for my trip.

I knew the schools awarded sabbaticals to teachers who had taught seven years and wanted to do something different—some worthwhile project or research. I'd been there way over seven years and hadn't considered taking a year off with pay to do something else.

I thanked Mr. Willis and went to the gym for my first class. As the day went on, I did go to the main office and get the papers to fill out for a sabbatical. I wasn't at all sure this was what I should do, but why not at least fill out the forms?

At home that night, I began to wonder just how I was going to finance this trip I was so sure I was to take. My house was mortgaged and my savings low. I guessed maybe God would help me sell my home to cover the expenses. I felt He would have a plan if I was doing His business.

The days that followed were busy. I was trying to end my school year as I learned more about where I was going, when I would go, and what I was getting into.

The following week, I heard His Voice. Clearly He said, *Go to Seattle, and get your vaccinations today.* I called in to take a day of personal leave and headed for King County Medical Services.

The first nurse asked me where I was going.

"Around the world," I replied.

"Can you be a bit more specific?"

"I'm afraid not, because I haven't any idea where I'm going."

She quickly covered her shock with professional calm and said, "Well, we had better get started."

Everything came at once. Would I be going to Africa? Probably. Likely I would need a yellow fever inoculation then. "We don't give those shots here. They are only given at the military hospital. Oh! I see you are in luck. Today is the only day you can get yellow fever shots for the next three months."

I stood in awe. Apparently, I was right on schedule, even though the plan was unseen, unwritten, and unknown.

After receiving several necessary shots, I headed to the military hospital. By now my arms were hurting, and I was quite exhausted from all of the diseases that had entered my poor body. As I walked into the large waiting area of the next hospital, I was shocked to see over a hundred people also waiting for inoculations. I murmured a prayer—more like a moan—because I wasn't sure I could stand up that long. Just then a doctor walked through a door, looked straight at me, and said, "I'll take you first."

I began to thank the Lord. He knew I was speechless, weary, and very aware of His intervention. As I drove the twenty miles back home from Seattle, I was more aware than ever that He was leading me. If I kept obeying, I could count on His faithfulness. Tears filled my eyes, and that night, blessed sleep restored me.

4

Looking Back and Looking Forward

I GREW UP IN Southern Alberta, Canada. We were a poor farm family, grateful for gardens, chickens, and a few fruit trees. Dad and Mom emigrated north from Oregon in the 1920s with the promise of cheap land to farm. The Depression was just beginning to show itself in the rearview mirror, and we kids didn't even know how poor we were.

One day, as we were out playing, I started to boast to my little neighbor friends that when I grew up, I was going to own a great, big white house. It would have many big rooms and even two indoor bathrooms. To me, that was almost beyond imagination. After all, our simple farmhouse had two bedrooms downstairs and an upstairs loft for seven children. No one I knew had indoor plumbing. Of course, my friends challenged me, making fun of my boasting. I often wondered why I made up such a whopper; it embarrassed me enough that I never forgot it.

Fast-forward to many years later: I had just finished my seventeenth year of teaching when I noticed a new housing development being built near my apartment in Auburn, Washington. I love to watch progress, so I often drove over to watch the new neighborhood take shape. As the community developed, I saw that nearly all the smaller houses were being quickly snapped up by eager buyers. Yet there was one very large house that just would not sell. I even prayed that the Lord would sell it to some nice family, but it just sat there. Just for fun, one day I walked through it. It was big: three bedrooms upstairs, a full, unfinished basement, and two fireplaces—there was space everywhere.

A Realtor met me during my walk-through, so I asked why the developer had built such a big house when all the others were bungalows. She said the builder had planned to live in it but now was constructing on another site. She asked if I wanted to buy it. I assured her I was single, and it was way too much house for me. Still, the idea stuck. I finally mentioned the house to my roommate, a fellow teacher, and asked what she thought of buying a house.

Her comeback was immediate. "If you buy that place, I'm not moving!" She was convinced no man would ever consider marrying a single girl who was living in a great big house. That was discouraging, but the idea of being a first-time homeowner would not leave my mind. I started to search for something smaller, but after a few weeks of looking, nothing seemed right. Was God leading me toward that enormous house? Once again, I slowly drove past that big house. I looked, I prayed some more, and I did another walk-through.

My dad taught me I would never have much unless I invested in something. He always felt a home provided a good financial security blanket. Could that be true for this single schoolteacher?

That next week, I again returned to the big white house with blue shutters. I really disliked those robin's-egg-blue shutters. The Realtor tracked my progress and saw my sales resistance weakening. "You can always paint those shutters," she suggested.

It was late one Sunday afternoon when I finally felt the eternal go-ahead that it was right to sign papers. I steadfastly refused, though, much to the saleslady's alarm, saying I would not do business on

Sunday. She warned me that someone else could easily come in and give her a down payment. My answer was simple. "Then let it go. God can keep it for me if He wants me to have it."

I went back to my apartment, confident of my decision. For the hundredth time, I turned it all over to the Lord. The next afternoon, I signed the papers, and to my amazement, my roommate of five years made the move with me. She and two other gals joined me in that very big white house.

Those women paid rent that covered the monthly mortgage payment while I used my teaching salary to furnish my new home. After two years, my roommates moved on, and I was left alone in that large house. I was surprised one day when my postman knocked on the door and asked if he could talk to me.

Don was a young widower, raising a growing daughter who was in my physical education classes. June was a total delight and often walked with me when I went to the tennis courts. We became friends, and I really enjoyed her delightful personality. I knew Don only as a nice guy who delivered mail and as the dad of an exceptional child. Now, here he was at my doorstep. Don told me he was a builder on the side and wondered if he could complete my unfinished basement for me. When I moved in, it was nothing more than studs.

His request really shocked me, so I questioned his generosity. He said that since his wife passed, June had just been lost. "She really loves you," he continued, "and I would very much enjoy doing something special to show my appreciation."

Don began to come over often to finish my daylight basement. My house now had five bedrooms, three baths, two fireplaces, and a big recreation room for my ever-growing home group. June went on to high school, and my world began to change.

By now I had twenty-one years of teaching under my belt. It was time to consider my alternatives: did I want to teach PE and art for another twenty years, or did I want to do something on the mission field? I always thought I would go do some sort of mission work one day, but what? I began to pray and ask Father.

One day, as I was praying, the Lord reminded me of my child-hood boast—the big white house, one that even had two indoor bathrooms. Now here I was, living in that dream house. Not only did God hear my boast, but He *fulfilled* it. What if God had much more in store for me than I could imagine? I wanted to know my Lord in a far deeper way.

> Let us acknowledge the LORD;
> let us press on to acknowledge him.
> As surely as the sun rises,
> he will appear;
> he will come to us like the winter rains,
> like the spring rains that water the earth.

—HOSEA 6:3 (NIV)

5

TOKYO AND KOREA

FIRST WORLD TRIP

As I walked down the red carpet to our jumbo jet heading for Tokyo, my heart was beating fast, and I was also a bit fearful. I was really on the way! This was the first leg of a journey that was to change my life. I was discovering that God could and would lead me on a new path.

I'm sure no one was ever as unprepared for a trip around the world as I was that crisp summer morning leaving Seattle. My seat-mate asked where I was going, and my reply left her eyes wide open. She peppered me with questions.

"You are going around the world?"

"Yes, I'm off to tell God's people how much He loves them." That opened a door for more conversation, making it easy to tell her of His love for her too. After that encounter, my heart was full of joy and peace; God was indeed going before me.

Tokyo was my first stop, and my college friend, June, was there to meet my plane. I stayed with her for a week, and during that short time, she introduced me to a multitude of people in the midst of that crowded Asian city. I had traveled to Europe years earlier, but wasn't all that interested in the cathedrals and castles I had seen there. I so needed June's introduction to the Orient. The crush of the masses on the train rides, the squat toilets, strange food, language barriers, and noise—everywhere I went, I was pushed and mauled. Culture shock set in fast.

June introduced me to many busy teachers and missionary children. Life was fast paced, and I'm sure I wasn't much of an encouragement. In fact, I merely tried to adjust and not need an encourager myself! I had so much to learn. If I accomplished anything in Japan, it was certainly by God's grace alone, working through His trusted servant June.

Just as I got my bearings in Tokyo and recovered from jet lag, I was saying good-bye and landing in South Korea. My next assignment was to visit a girls' high school there. Part of the agreement for fulfilling my sabbatical requirements was to compare US educational programs with those in other countries. This would be my first experience teaching outside of America; I was to compare facilities, curriculum, and students and then send reports back to my school in Washington.

Pusan was where my Korean school was located, in the southern part of the country. I saw a huge sports field there, with lots of children all dressed in white uniforms as they did drills and learned how to jump hurdles. There were also many girls learning medical procedures. They told me there was a very real threat of invasion from North Korea, so all the girls were trained to administer IVs, dress wounds, and work with stretchers. I was very impressed.

One afternoon, the principal took me aside to share a miracle story about the school. It was a story of a marvelous blessing of provision from the Lord. This school was praying for a solution to their need for more space. The Korean government regulations for space required per child had forced the school to limit its enrollment. South Korea sits on a mountain range; flat space was minimal. The school had built to the very edges of their property and had already made a play space on the roof of their eight-story classroom building. What was the school to do?

All the faculty joined together, requesting help from the Lord. Children from all over the area dreamed of attending a Christian school with their high standards, but there was no room for more students. One day, Doris, the principal, received a call from the city council, requesting a meeting. Three city employees came to her office to explain their problem. The city was growing very fast, they said. The engineers and city planners needed space to build a freeway around Pusan, South Korea's second-largest city. The problem was that they needed to find materials for this huge job. The group laid out their plan and then presented their question. Could the city buy the mountain the school sat on? They wanted the rock and dirt the school had. They promised to flatten the area after removing the mountain so another tall building could be added, as well as play areas for more children. What a solution! Our Father provided the answer for the city while providing a future school building for over five hundred girls.

All praise to the King! Right where I stood there had been a literal mountain, now flattened. I looked around at the building and play area that now existed. I was reminded of Zechariah 4:7 (NIV): "What are you, mighty mountain? …you will become level ground."

This school was made up of senior-high students who were grouped by their scholastic records. This particular one had only children in the low-A and high-B levels, so competition was intense. I would have never qualified to attend that school when I was their age!

My classes had over fifty students each. Their names were written in Korean script, so I could not decipher a single word. Each girl wore an identical hairstyle—black bangs with a short bob. Their uniforms were navy blue and white, so to me, they all looked like cute penguins as they sat together, two at a desk. *Jesus, help me!* was my silent cry, and He did, by sending a young male Korean teacher who spoke English. Peter was also a Christian; he rescued me from that cultural challenge and became a special friend.

As my days there turned into weeks, I began to see many differences in American and Korean schools. The classroom windows were covered with tissue paper so there would be no distractions. The ceilings were ten to twelve feet high with single lightbulbs dimly lighting the spaces, making the rooms seem like dark and dreary prisons. There were no wall decorations, posters, charts, or teaching tools. I marveled that those students learned *anything*. What could I do with a blackboard and a piece of chalk? I started to pray.

Discipline was extreme from my American perspective. Often students started arriving at school by 6:00 a.m. and kept on studying until after 6:00 p.m. There was a terrible fear of failing, and losing face was the worst thing that could happen in that culture.

As an exhorter (one of the thinking styles God gives—exhorters are the encouragers of the body of Christ; see Romans 12) from America whose life goal was to have a good time, I managed to loosen up my classes a bit. In fact, I was far too loose for the Korean system. On my final day, as I left the school, all the young girls I had taught opened the classroom windows and tried to peek out as they shouted in accented English, "Good-bye, Teacher!" They had responded to my freer ways of teaching; things would get back to normal when I moved on. I was sad to leave them, but other countries beckoned.

My Lord knows the way through the wilderness,
All I have to do is follow.

WORDS AND MUSIC BY SIDNEY E. COX

6

GOD AND BOEING IN SEOUL

Those six weeks in Pusan really made me miss hearing the English language. Listening to a foreign language all day long can wear you out! Someone in Pusan told me I could meet a wonderful pastor who would introduce me to several other pastors if I would attend the World Conference of the Assembly of God leaders in Seoul. This sounded like a welcome change. It had been a real challenge to teach physical education to young girls who only spoke Korean; I was often reduced to sign language to give my instructions. A week away in Seoul seemed like a great prospect--maybe I could meet some Americans and have a break.

I caught an early-morning flight from Pusan to Seoul, but when I arrived in the capital city, there was no one to meet me. I waited for a long time, but no one came. Where was Pastor Oh? The airport had almost emptied out when an English-speaking man approached me and asked if he could help. He told me which bus to catch for a ride near the convention center, where the world conference was being held. I gratefully left the airport, but wondered how I would ever meet up with Pastor Oh. Our only plan was to meet at the airport.

Soon, I found myself in a huge city packed with tourists. People came from around the world to take part in these meetings and had made their plans months earlier. I went to the first hotel I could find and was told they were fully booked. I asked if they could please call around and see if there was a room elsewhere. They were kind and tried, but every other hotel had the same response: they were full to overflowing. I had no idea what to do. No one in the world knew where I was. When I told God I wanted someone to go with me on this adventure, He had promised that He would be that Someone. This would be a good time for Him to show up! I took a seat in the lobby and began to pray, hoping He would lead me.

After a long time, I felt maybe I should get some coffee. I lugged my suitcase onto the elevator and headed toward the coffee shop. As I looked around at the others in the elevator, I saw one other pale face. Thankfully, she was an American. I asked if I could buy her a cup of coffee, and she accepted. We chatted, and I told her my dilemma. She felt sure she could get me a room and headed back to the front desk to plead my case. Back to the lobby I went and waited to be called up to the desk with news of a room for me.

My new friend, Maureen, went back to her room, confident that I would soon get a room as well. Hours later, she was back in the lobby and shocked to see me still there. Once again she marched up to the front desk, demanding a place for me. She returned to me and told me to come up to her room, where the front desk would call when mine was ready. I was shocked by her boldness but gladly accepted her invitation.

Up to the penthouse we went! What a view of Seoul she had. While I was looking out, I asked Maureen about a beautiful building I saw very near the hotel. She told me it was the Taiwan Embassy. I was amazed to see this place. Others had encouraged me to include Taiwan in my travels, but without a visa, I decided to just skip it and continue on to the Philippines. Now all I had to do was walk across the street, and I could have a visa in my passport. With nothing else to do, it seemed like God was clearly telling me that Taiwan was on His itinerary for me.

Hours later, when I returned to my new friend's room with a visa for Taiwan, Maureen happily announced that my room was now ready. What? How did she manage that? Over another cup of coffee, she explained that her husband headed up Boeing in Korea, and that Boeing owned that very hotel. When her husband called and asked for a room, somehow one was made available. Since I was a teacher from Auburn, Washington, and they were from Renton, the next town over, they felt they had helped a friend from home. And they had!

Oh, my, I was so impressed with Father's care for His child. The conference was excellent. I enjoyed a trip to Pastor Oh's church of ten thousand people and met a man from Detroit who gave me instructions on how to stop there on my way home to pick up a new car; I would need one to replace the car I'd sold. And now I was on my way to Taiwan; once again, I had seen God at work on my behalf.

> The steps of a good man are ordered by the LORD
> and he delights in his way.
>
> —Psalm 37:23 NKJV

> All the way my Savior leads me;
> What have I to ask beside?
> Can I doubt His tender mercy,
> Who through life has been my Guide?
> Heav'nly peace, divinest comfort,
> Here by faith in Him to dwell!

For I know, whate'er befall me,
Jesus doeth all things well;
For I know, whate'er befall me,
Jesus doeth all things well.

—"ALL THE WAY MY SAVIOR LEADS ME" BY FANNY
J. CROSBY, 1875

7

Learning to Praise through Rejection

Taiwan

MY NEXT FLIGHT took me to Taichung, Taiwan. Taichung was small by Asian standards, only about two million people, and there was a school there for children of missionaries. For me, it was an introduction to some very challenging heartaches and a horrifying experience—being kicked out of a missionary guesthouse. This was not how I had hoped my ministry to missionaries would turn out!

I was asked to share at a meeting my first night in Taichung. My topic was "Praise—Especially When You Don't Feel Like It." That was the lesson God was teaching me, so I wanted to share this fresh bread with His people. It was taken from 1 Thessalonians 5:18: "In every thing give thanks, for this is the will of God in Christ Jesus concerning you." The people seemed to respond well to my message, and I was glad to fall into bed that night, exhausted after both international travel and ministry.

By morning, I was refreshed and ready to meet more folks. Going in to breakfast, I was totally unprepared for my encounter with a very angry house manager. She greeted me coldly and announced that as soon as breakfast was over, she expected me to pack my bags and move out. I had no idea what was wrong. I tried to ask her, but her only response was that I had no right to teach about praise. She was so angry that no other words would come.

The night before, I'd accepted an invitation to teach at a women's Bible study that morning; a missionary was coming by to get me immediately after breakfast. I ate humble pie and asked if I could leave my things in the room until lunch was over. She reluctantly agreed, so I packed my suitcase and left it sitting by the front door. My heart was heavy; I was humiliated and embarrassed.

On our way to the morning Bible study, I asked my driver if the guesthouse hostess had an anger problem or if it was just me. He told me of several of her outbursts and that his wife dreaded even going to the guesthouse. No one knew why, but it seemed that everyone who came in contact with this missionary lady got wounded.

Our morning session was a great time of fellowship around God's Word. When my driver, a missionary himself, returned to pick me up to take me back to the guesthouse, he asked if I had taught again that morning. "Yes," I replied. His eyes teared up.

"Why do the women get all the fresh teaching?" he said. "We men need it too."

I had no real answer, except that I had been invited to a women's meeting. I had no idea how to respond, but the Lord had been dealing with me on this matter of women teaching men. As we drove back to the guesthouse, the Lord spoke to my heart. *Why don't you invite men to your meetings? I asked you to go tell My people I love them. I also love the men.* That day, God settled it in my heart: I'd never worry about defending my calling again. He would be my defense. Ever since, by God's grace, I have been free to minister to any and all who are eager to listen.

We pulled into the guesthouse driveway. I had no idea where to go, but I sure knew I was not welcome to stay there. As quietly as possible, I went to pay my bill, looking for someone who might suggest where I should stay next.

Just then, an angry female voice commanded me to come into the office. It was the guesthouse manager. I fearfully obeyed, only to hear her announce that I wasn't supposed to go anywhere else. She had called her boss, who flatly refused to allow her to make a guest leave. Furthermore, I could stay all week if I wanted.

Now what to do? I was not excited about staying somewhere I wasn't wanted. I meekly returned to my room and unpacked. "Father, what are You up to?"

Later that afternoon, I forced myself to go to the living room area of the guesthouse. Once again, I heard the angry voice. "Come in here!" she demanded.

I am sure the courage I had to obey came directly from God. I walked into her office, where she politely asked me to sit down and listen. As I did, I heard the inner cry of a lost, lonely, broken heart. Joan began by saying, "There is no way I can praise a God who let my young son die on foreign soil."

As she wept out her anger and bitterness, my heart ached for this hurting lady. No parent wants to bury a child. We talked, but mostly I listened, prayed, and sought guidance. The old hymn came to mind: "Farther along you'll know all about it, farther along, you'll understand why."[1] I stayed in her office a long time that afternoon and spent time with her on two more afternoons before my departure time came around. As I looked back on that trying time, I was grateful for being able to help shoulder Joan's hurt. My true joy came later as my driver, the same missionary who had served me earlier, took me to the airport. He reported the change his wife had experienced in Joan's attitude; his wife even felt that she could now return to the missionary guesthouse.

---

1 "Farther Along," by Rev. W. A. Fletcher, ca. 1911.

From Taiwan to Manila, Philippines, isn't a long journey, but it did give me time to reflect and ask Father for a deeper love for His hurting children. No wonder He told me they needed to be reminded of His heart for them.

> I will extol the LORD at all times;
> his praise will always be on my lips.
> I will glory in the LORD;
> let the afflicted hear and rejoice.
> Glorify the LORD with me;
> let us exalt his name together.
> I sought the LORD, and he answered me;
> he delivered me from all my fears.
> Those who look to him are radiant;
> their faces are never covered with shame.
> This poor man called, and the LORD heard him;
> he saved him out of all his troubles.

PSALM 34:1–6 (NIV)

8

First Time in Manila

There are only 624 nautical miles between the northern island of the Philippines and Taiwan. Some Filipinos joke that you can hear a cock crow in Taiwan when you are at the northernmost point of their country. Still, each Asian country has its own culture; orderly Japan and Taiwan did not prepare me for the Philippines.

Walking outside the Manila airport brought me to a mass of shouting, pressing, demanding, begging, pushing, and pulling people. It seemed like everyone vied for my attention. Some tried to take my picture. Others tried to sell me their trinkets or get me into their taxi, and everyone wanted my money! I tried to pull my luggage away from five or six kids who worked just as hard to separate it from my grip. It shocked me to see so many people trying to earn a few pesos by helping me. I kept scanning the crowds, looking for my contact, a light-skinned man I'd never met.

I had made plans to have someone pick me up and take me to Faith Academy when my plane landed in Manila. To my great relief, I spotted a tall American towering over the shorter Filipinos. He took charge and led me through the crowds to his car. I sure was glad to meet this friendly missionary. His name was Don, and he was the high school principal at Faith Academy. Soon, his wife welcomed me with a friendly hug. Almost before I had my bags out of their car, Don left for a meeting. His wife, Nan, was already late for her Bible study, so there I was in their charming house, left alone with their house girl.

Grace, their Filipina helper, was God's gift to me. She introduced me to mission work with the nationals and truly lived up to her name again and again. It was obvious that I was not the first bedraggled, foreign houseguest she'd ever welcomed, as she knew exactly what to do with me. She insisted I must be tired from my journey and kindly suggested I lay down for a rest. She brought me a delicious, cool *calamansi* (a fruit like a small lime) drink that was so refreshing. What a nice welcome to my new country. I had no idea at that time that Grace was to become a lifelong friend and wonderful missionary herself, as years later she became a part of the Precious Jewels staff with our friends Lorrie and Joke.

Rest was followed by dinner and more time with my vibrant hosts. They outlined what my next few days at Faith Academy would look like. After a few wonderful days with this couple, they left for a conference, and I moved to a room at a missionary guesthouse in Quezon City, down the hill and through unspeakable traffic.

At that time, Faith was a Christian school that was home to nearly five hundred students from missionary families working all over Asia. Many international oil companies' employees living in the Philippines also sent their children to this fine Christian school, perched high on a hill that overlooked the city. Children were bussed from all over the sprawling city of Manila.

Traffic was a shock to me, as five million people struggled to reach their various destinations on foot or by tricycle, motorcycle, car, jeepney, or bus. There were even a few horses pulling small carts. My time that day at the school was filled with school staff and gaining understanding of the Philippine mission work. I was asked to lead the teachers' morning devotional time the next several days.

It was a blistering-hot day as I headed out one morning to fulfill that assignment. That was not unusual, but the rainy season added terrible flooding to the moist heat. There was much floating debris, and steamy mist arose over all the puddles and streets. I had boarded an old school bus filled with chattering children that headed slowly to Faith Academy.

As we made our way through the hot, crowded streets, I could not detect any reasonable traffic rules. Later, I was told that if you ended up in traffic court because of an accident, the first question asked was, "Did you apply the horn?" It seemed to me that people drove with one foot on the accelerator and one hand on the horn. Jeepney drivers prided themselves in not just blasting horns, but horns that played a whole phrase of loud music. And jeepneys were the most popular means of public transport in the country. Originally made from US military jeeps left there after World War II, they were known for their colorful decoration and crowded seating.

As the kids and I were waiting in yet another traffic jam, I again looked out the bus window. When I saw the mud holes filled with filth, children playing in the muck, and needs everywhere, my heart filled with despair. How could any one person make a difference in this place?

Just then, my eyes caught a very unusual thing. There in the midst of all the misery was a snow-white lily that had pushed up through the mud. It was spotless—fresh, clean, and beautiful. I marveled at the unbelievable sight. How had it managed to bloom and stay white with all that mud completely surrounding it?

Then I was given the answer to my wondering and discouragement. Jesus showed me that He was like that lovely lily—always fresh, clean, and so very beautiful. He could be the hope, light, and source of strength for all those lost souls. Just as impossible as that lily blooming perfectly in the midst of hopelessness, Jesus could come right there and make something wonderful out of all the trials of their lives.

I had my fresh devotional message for that morning: Jesus is always the hope we can depend on. He makes all things beautiful in His time (Eccl. 3:11), and He assures us that what is coming is far greater than we can ever imagine.

> But as it is written: "Eye has not seen, nor ear heard, nor have entered into the heart of man the things which God has prepared for those who love Him." But God has revealed them to us through His Spirit. For the Spirit searches all things, yes, the deep things of God.
>
> —1 Corinthians 2:9–10 (NKJV)

9

ART FOR MISSIONS

MY TIME IN Manila sealed my love for the Filipino people, but now I was off to Singapore.

The contrast could not have been greater from what looked like chaos to near perfection. Here was an international airport that promised to have you out of the door, baggage in hand, in less than twenty minutes. Wide-open boulevards with orchids growing everywhere amazed me. When we left Manila, it took over two hours just to clear the air traffic and climb into the sky. Now, I was in a tiny country kept prosperous and orderly by tight Chinese rule.

The only place I knew to stay was the Raffles Hotel, made famous by Ernest Hemingway. It was very British and was run like a higher class western hotel. It was a part of the Fairmont Hotel chain, so though it was smaller, it reminded me of the impressive Empress Hotel in Victoria, BC.

My room looked very nice for an older hotel room, but I woke up in the middle of the night to a bad surprise. A tropical rainstorm was raging outside, and my ceiling was dripping in three different places. My frantic call to the front desk brought a crisp apology and led to the delivery of three buckets to catch the leaks. They assured me the leaks would be fixed the next day.

The next morning the heavy rainstorm was just a memory. Sitting one-degree north of the equator made the island nation a tropical paradise, so after breakfast, I joined many of the guests around the swimming pool. When I was asked by another guest what brought me to Singapore, I told her I was headed around the world to tell people God loved them. That puzzled her. She wanted to know what exactly I was going to tell these people. I wasn't sure what she was asking, really, so she rephrased her question. "What do you think is more important, that you tell people how to meet God or that you provide food and clothing for the starving that don't know Him? Which is more important?" It was easy to see that she was trying to make a point and that we were coming from different places in our opinions.

I proceeded to tell her that in the long run, definitely, salvation was the most important. Although I knew that without compassion, there would be little possibility of needy people receiving truth.

She said, "I, too, am giving people a message, but my message is to feed and clothe the needy that are in the world today." We soon parted ways, wishing each other the very best. I didn't feel that I answered her well, but I also didn't know how I could have responded differently.

Not trusting that my room would see repairs that day, I followed a suggestion to go to a motel not too far away that was new and nice. It wasn't the great Raffles, but there were no middle-of-the-night surprises!

After getting settled in my new location, I took the address that was given to me in Manila and headed off in a taxi to meet a Christian brother and visit a ministry I thought would be very interesting. Fos had been a teacher of art; I had a minor in art and taught art for five years, so I wondered how he was using this talent for the Lord.

Fos taught classes of three to five men who were learning how to paint scenery on oil canvases. These were very talented students, so with Fos's coaching, these men painted for a living. He developed their skills in marketing as well as sales. As they worked, they were paid an hourly wage while he looked for ways to expand the market for sales. Along with their art and marketing lessons, they also learned about Jesus and His plan for their lives. For several years after that trip, I bought and sold the work of these budding artists and sent back dollars to support them. I had no idea that our lives would intertwine years later back in chaotic Manila.

My next destination was Kuala Lumpur.

10

MALAYSIA/KUALA LUMPUR

I HAD PLANS TO go to a prestigious high school for missionary kids in Malaysia, but the school was closed for Christmas vacation. I was blessed with an invitation from a lady who was the principal of another school in Kuala Lumpur. It was a school for the elite, with this Malay Christian as its principal. Betty invited me to stay at her home over the holidays; not only was she a very strong Christian, but she was also a top educator and wonderful hostess. I loved the way the houses there had walls that could open like enormous windows. I still chuckle remembering a huge frog jumping through her house from one end to the other. I was reading my Bible early one morning when a big frog hopped right by. It was quite a shock!

Because Muslims were in control of the Malay government, this country followed Muslim rules in all of its schools. I'd never experienced anything like that. The main ethnic group in Malaysia was Malay, with Chinese in second place. (One thing you learn from traveling in Asia is that there are Chinese people in every country.) By law, Chinese children could be taught Christianity, but Malay children were not to be converted. Much pressure was put on the school principal to personally convert to Islam. This faithful Christian woman was harassed, bribed, and called on the carpet to no avail; her faith never wavered.

Betty's school was known for its outstanding performance in every field. It seemed every important leader in Kuala Lumpur wanted his children to attend her school, and because the school had such a great reputation, the Muslim pressure wasn't strong enough to close down her work. This brave woman continued to reach the children of the Chinese leaders of the country, and the Christian children then evangelized their friends, regardless of the rules of the officials.

I was delighted to meet all these schoolgirls and to share my testimony with this group of outstanding future leaders of Malaysia. At the conclusion of my visit, which lasted a week, I led a weekend retreat for the students during their Christmas break. The speaker they planned on canceled at the last minute, so I was glad to fill in. Maybe this was the reason I had been sent to Malaysia. I had to be very careful not to indoctrinate the Malay children, or I would have been quickly ushered out of the country. The girls with Chinese or Indian backgrounds, however, were fair game and wonderfully open.

The night before I left, I heard four-part harmony coming from outside our home. I peeked into the darkness and saw the schoolgirls, lit candles in their hands, singing beautiful Christmas carols for us. What a wonderful Christmas present from my loving Father. I was far from home but not out of His care.

But in your hearts revere Christ as Lord. Always be prepared to give an answer to everyone who asks you to give the reason for the hope that you have. But do this with gentleness and respect.

—1 Peter 3:15 (NIV)

11

SRI LANKA

I HAD NO PLANS to go to Sri Lanka. The stack of tickets I had in my hand as I left SeaTac Airport did not include this small island country off the coast of India. My idea was to go directly from India to Africa. My ticket from Malaysia took me from India right to East Africa. The travel agent who helped me chart my course around the world did not foresee an airline strike that literally closed India to air travel, so my diversion took me to this beautiful tropical island called Sri Lanka. The routing gave me a twelve-hour layover in the capital of Colombo before the flight continued on to the Seychelles Islands and then directly to Nairobi, Kenya.

I had never wanted to go to India in the first place. In my mind, India was a country crawling with ants—it had so many people! Even though this new routing took me to locations I had never heard of, I was relieved to avoid the masses of India. Sri Lanka may not have been on my itinerary, but the Holy Spirit knew I needed to be there for an important connection.

Inside the Sri Lankan air terminal, many others crowded passport control, and I was quickly maneuvered out of place in the line.

Suddenly, a very strong voice said on my behalf, "That lady was ahead of you—it's her turn."

I was embarrassed, and so was the rude traveler who had stepped in front of me. He quickly took his place behind me while I was given a day pass to see the city. I thanked my advocate, and she proceeded to direct me on through Customs. We began to talk, and I learned she had an important job in the German Ministry of Commerce. Gertrude said she was going to sleep for a while, but if I wanted, we could meet later for dinner before I had to return for my ongoing flight. That sounded good; I was always eager for some good conversation in English.

The airport where I had met my new friend was far from the city of Colombo. I rented a small sleeping room in the airport to try to get some rest, but sleep wouldn't come, so I left my travel bags there and went off to explore the city.

My bus ride to Colombo was almost entirely through thick jungle. By the time I boarded the shuttle, nearly all the other travelers had gone on ahead of me to the city, so the bus was almost empty.

I must have dozed off in the tropical heat when I suddenly felt the bus jerk to a stop. I looked up, and there was a large elephant standing in front of us, filling the entire road. The mammoth creature didn't seem to be agitated, just curious. He wandered around the bus and put his trunk inside my open window. I wasn't afraid—he seemed to want to smell me. I tried to get a picture of him, but all that turned out was a close-up of the end of his trunk. He pulled his trunk out of the window and wandered off back into the jungle. I'd never been that close to any wild beast before, but I was suddenly very wide awake!

The shuttle dropped me off in the capital city, where I had ten hours on my hands. What to do? I took a long walk and saw some real characters. One man was dressed so unusually I asked if I could take his picture. He was flattered and then furious because he wanted to be paid. I decided I'd better stay near the beautiful hotel where I was to meet Gertrude and try to keep out of trouble! I got a really nice haircut there and discovered why Ceylon tea was the best in the world. Who knew that this tiny country was the world's largest exporter of tea?

I sat in the lovely gardens of the hotel and enjoyed my tea. Now I had time to pray. Was this meeting with Gertrude an opportunity from the Lord? I sure prayed it would be. She met me in the lobby a few hours later, and we ate a delicious meal at the hotel restaurant.

We chatted about her job. She often traveled internationally, was very busy, and attended lots of meetings. Finally, she asked what I was doing so far from Seattle. I began to tell her about the Lord and His call to let people know He loved them. She listened, asked a few questions, and listened some more. I realized this spiritual talk about Jesus was all new to her. I saw a hungry heart and was sorry it was time for me to head back to the airport. Gertrude gave me her card and asked me to look her up when I came through Europe on my way home.

It was dark by now, and I had to take a taxi back to the airport. Once again, Gertrude acted as my protector, talking to the driver and letting him know she was writing down his cab number to make sure he delivered me safely to my destination.

Almost as soon as we left the hotel, we were in the jungle again on small, winding roads. That was when I noticed the taxi moving slower and slower till we were traveling at a snail's pace. About five minutes later, the driver rolled to a complete stop as he parked by a small grass hut. I could hear vulgar sounds and loud noises that seemed to be coming from a drunken crowd. To make matters worse, the driver got out without saying a word and headed in, leaving me alone in the dark in the backseat of his cab.

I began to pray and finally realized just how dangerous this could be. Here I was, a very white American woman, sitting alone in a rattletrap of a car in the middle of the night in a Sri Lankan jungle. I had a purse and camera on my lap and a small carry-on bag beside me. How much was my life worth to the people behind the door of this hut, where the loud music and laughter of heavy drinkers filled the air? All I could see in the darkness was one small, dim light illuminating the front door.

I began to pray much harder. It didn't comfort me to realize that no one in the world knew where I was. The air strike had changed my plans, and nobody even knew I was in a country they'd likely never heard of.

In the midst of these fearful thoughts, the Lord gave me a picture. It was almost an out-of-body experience as He showed me looking down on myself in the backseat of this old car. There I sat, hands crossed in my lap, looking like a nice, calm lady. "Dear Jesus," I prayed, "keep these men pure in thought, and bring my driver back!"

After what seemed like ages, my driver did return alone. I gruffly told him that he would have to hurry, or I would miss my plane. He nodded, and we slowly headed toward the airport. Was I ever relieved when I saw the welcoming airport lights.

As my plane cut through the night over the Indian Ocean, I began to see just how faithful Father had been to me. I closed my eyes to sleep with tears of joy running down my cheeks. My heart was full. The Lord told me I would get to know Him better on this trip around the world. I didn't know that a Sri Lankan jungle would be a part of that plan!

My plane from Sri Lanka took me to the Seychelles Islands. As far as you could see, there was water, the Indian Ocean, but when I arrived, it was night, so the view was an open heaven. It was a beautiful, starry night—stars everywhere, with no artificial light to dim God's lights from above. It would be one of my most unusual Christmas Eve experiences.

I met many missionaries who served in the Seychelles with Far East Broadcasting Company. Their challenge was to get the gospel into India and China. China was very closed to the gospel, but God was sending radio waves across the Indian Ocean, and the message was getting into and across the vast country of India. I was thrilled to see the way He was working and the dedication of those faithful workers.

While there, I met a British school administrator named Helen. She invited me to come meet her students in Kenya and see her all-girls secondary school. Kenya had very few secondary schools for girls at that time, and I was eager for the opportunity to visit hers. I could write a report on my observations there that would help fulfill my sabbatical obligations.

I spent four days in the Seychelles and, at Helen's invitation, got a reservation to fly to Nairobi with her. We agreed that I would come visit her school the following week.

> Show me your ways, O LORD; teach me your paths;
> guide me in your truth and teach me, for you are
> God my Savior,
> and my hope is in you all day long.
>
> —PSALM 25:4–5 (NIV)

12

A WORD FROM THE LORD

HELEN'S AFRICA

ONE PERSON I felt I should visit before I started my journey around the world was my college roommate and longtime friend Fran. Her journey into a deeper walk with God really fascinated me; I knew she had a walk with Jesus unlike mine, and I wanted to learn more from her.

As I pulled into Fran's driveway, I was greeted by a host of young children who seemed to be everywhere at once. Fran and Russ had adopted six hard-to-place orphans from many backgrounds. I knew a bit of their story, and it always challenged me how Fran managed the troop she called her "gang."

Following the excitement of greeting company, Fran sent the gang outside to play, and we sat down to get caught up on each other's lives. After a great time of sharing, as I prepared to leave, Fran asked if I'd like her to pray for me. I agreed. My experience with the gift of prophecy and a word of knowledge was limited; I was more a doubter than a believer. I wasn't against these new insights; I just hadn't seen them at work in my own life. Fran, though, had jumped into these gifts of the Spirit with both feet and was using them regularly.

As Fran prayed for me, those gifts of the Holy Spirit came through her words. She began to say that on my travels, God was going to open doors to some very important people from many different nations, and I was going to witness to them for Him.

I don't recall what other words came through Fran's mouth, but that statement went deep into my heart, and I never forgot it. That said, I didn't seek to fulfill those words or even think about them until I was halfway around the world.

My travels had now taken me to Africa for the first time. The brick-red soil worn smooth by bare feet gave me a strong awareness of the poverty just outside Kenya's capital city of Nairobi. People in the countryside worked hard, seemed to sing continually, and appeared happier than those I met in the crushing crowds of Nairobi.

Helen's school was about twenty miles from Nairobi, and was full of beautiful young women in blue-and-white uniforms. The rules and strict order she upheld really challenged me. My classes at home were full of free-thinking gals with boyfriends foremost on their minds; here across the globe, study, work, and long hours of homework filled the students' days. Perfection was demanded, both in their dress and in daily responsibilities.

I wanted everyone to loosen up, but this was no leisurely school system. Parents had sacrificed greatly just to get their daughters into secondary classes, so everyone worked hard with no nonsense. I spent a week with Helen and could easily see we were miles apart in how we approached education, even as we started a comfortable friendship. As she drove me to the airport for my next stop, Ethiopia, I knew I'd miss this new friend. I told her if she ever got to America, to look me up. Little did I know that God would use that casual invitation to bring us together down the road as ministry partners in North America.

> Teach me to do Your will, for you are my God;
> may your good Spirit lead me on level ground.

> —Psalm 143:10 (NIV)

13

TAFFARA DEGUEFE AND THE ETHIOPIAN UPRISING

USE MY NAME

I FIRST HEARD HIS name from my sister Grace. She was nine, and I was fourteen. Dad had taken me with him back to the US while my mother, younger sister, and older brothers were still living in Calgary. Dad was searching for work and a place for us to live so his wife and their daughter, Grace, could join us. I'm not sure I ever met Taffara DeGuefe in person, but I knew he was a college student from Ethiopia who was sent to Canada to be educated. Our church asked for a family to take in this young man.

Taffara's home in Calgary was with my mom's closest friend. Mrs. Allen hosted many of us for children's Bible classes, so I knew her well. She generously opened her home even wider as she welcomed this international student to stay with her. As I later heard the story of my younger sister and her friendship with Taffara, I learned it started with Grace's love for monkeys. Because Taffara was from Africa, she was *sure* he could get her a monkey to love. Grace stayed with Mrs. Allen and got acquainted with Taffara while our mom had an operation. He was a lonely young man far from home, so my sister soon filled a place in his heart. No monkey ever appeared, but a friendship began that lasted over seventy years.

I heard some of the stories he wrote to Grace during his amazing climb to a top position in Ethiopia. He became a head of banking and economic development for his beloved country; he remained humble and was loved by the elite as well as the poor.

When Grace, now a grandma, heard I was going to Africa on my world trip, she asked if I would try to look up her childhood friend Taffara. I wrote to him and made plans to meet him when I reached Ethiopia. God prepared an American school where I could stay while I visited Ethiopia's capital city of Addis Ababa.

I called Taffara's office and was delighted to hear he'd be glad to see me. The next morning, he called me to ask if I would come to his home for lunch the following day. He asked if I'd mind his driver coming by to pick me up. Taffara said there would be another passenger joining me for the ride, if that was OK. We agreed on times, and the plan was in place.

True to his word, a limousine arrived for me at the Christian school where I was volunteering. The other passenger was a very distinguished man, whom I learned was an ambassador from Uganda. I was very aware of his impeccable appearance as I glanced down at my well-worn cotton missionary dress.

When we arrived at Taffara's residence, I noticed there were several other cars—expensive cars—around the grounds. His home was beautiful, though conservative and modest. The spacious living room was filled with ambassadors from many countries in Africa. All had been invited to this luncheon. Taffara respectfully introduced me to his many influential friends, and I waited in anticipation to learn why he'd gathered us all there.

After lunch, he welcomed us and began to speak. "This is my friend from America," Taffara said, pointing to me. "I have asked all of you here to meet Esther. She is the ambassador of heaven—God's representative. I want her to share with us today."

I was very surprised! I had no idea he was going to ask me to share why I was in Ethiopia. I can't recall a thing I said, but I did remember the word of knowledge[1] that had been given to me before I left Seattle. God spoke through my friend Fran, who told me, "God will use you to minister to many influential leaders from many countries." I thought that was impossible. How could I, a lowly American schoolteacher, minister to powerful people from other countries? I dismissed it, sure it could never happen. My God was way too small.

Now the prophecy had come to pass, and I was ashamed of my lack of faith and awed by God's faithfulness. God gave me several opportunities to share more personally with individuals during the coffee hour that followed.

In the midst of this wonderful experience, I didn't realize how dangerous the city was becoming. I had no access to news, so I was quite ignorant of the growing tensions that led to Addis Ababa being taken over by a communist coup that very night. The street markets were in an uproar. The people were told they could not go outside, as some of their fellow countrymen were killed in the takeover.

Even BBC (British Broadcasting Corporation), the news source for much of the English-speaking world, was blacked out. Airlines halted all flights, and no one could go in or out of the country. Emperor Haile Selassie, thought by many to be their god, was under house arrest. I joined the missionaries in prayer where I was staying, gladly seeking God's protection and deliverance for us all.

The following morning, the travel ban was lifted, and we were free to move about. I had previously accepted a request to speak at a missionary meeting in downtown Addis that day. Several folks assured

---

1 First Corinthians 12:8 talks about the word of knowledge as one of the gifts of the Holy Spirit. A person functioning in that gift can speak things into another person's life about which they have no previous knowledge. Often, its purpose is to encourage and confirm, as it was in this case.

me it would be safe to go, so I took a public bus to town. I was the only white person on board; many stared at me and probably wondered what I was doing on public transportation in those very tense times.

I made it into town safely and walked up to the missionary compound where I'd been invited to speak. They had a huge wall around the campus and a strong steel gate large enough to let cars enter and leave. I was allowed in, but all was quiet when the gate closed quickly behind me. Still, I forgot the outside tensions and was busy teaching and ministering to about twenty-five guests. It was after 3:00 p.m. when I left and made my way down to the bus stop.

As I glanced around, I saw there were a lot of folks just wandering throughout the downtown square. I began to wonder why my bus hadn't arrived. I decided I'd better call a cab, but they, too, had stopped running. The air felt eerie and tense; things were too quiet for a bustling city.

The crowd began to press in, and I realized there were easily over a hundred people crowding in around me. I heard that precious green bean Voice firmly say, *Go back to the missionary center. Do not act fearful, be deliberate, and don't rush.* I obeyed, trying to appear calm on the outside as I returned to the high walls and iron gate of the missionary compound. I was well aware that I was on very dangerous ground. The walls didn't seem as safe as they had earlier, but once inside them, I was grateful for Christian companions.

I stayed in the compound until after dark, when a brave fellow said he would drive me back to the missionary school grounds where I was staying. He took a long way out of the city that felt safer than the shorter route. After what seemed like an eternity but was probably only an hour or so, I walked into the mission station where I had begun my day. A large group of missionaries got up from their knees and crowded around me. Was I OK? Had I been in danger? Where had I been? "We've all been praying for you to return."

Thank you, Jesus! The danger was far from over. I went to my room and again saw the strong hand of the Lord and His angels protecting me.

Early the next morning, I asked for directions to get to downtown Addis Ababa to visit Taffara at work. We were given clearance to proceed with our normal lives, so I went downtown as had been arranged.

The bus driver let me off right in front of a beautiful new bank with a large, imposing wall. The lawn was spacious, and flowers lined the entrance. This was by far the nicest building I'd seen since I'd arrived in Ethiopia.

When I entered the bank building and asked for directions to Taffara's office, I noted much hesitancy in the person I asked. I assured him I was told to come to Taffara's office when I arrived, so he directed me to the elevator and said to go to the top floor for more instructions.

At first, my elevator companions were friendly as we began our ascent, but they grew more and more uncomfortable with me as each floor passed, and I didn't get off. At last, I was alone and at the top. I went into a large, office-like room that was crowded with many secretaries, all very busy and intent on ignoring this strange woman. I waited and waited for someone to come see what I wanted. Finally, one did come to the counter and ask what I was there for. I said, "I have an appointment with Taffara, and he said to come to his office." Reluctantly, she led me past all the madly typing secretaries, who continued to act too busy to even look up. There was no missing that I was being purposely ignored.

Just as we turned a corner, there was the man. He stopped in his tracks, turned, and rushed over to us. He grasped my hands and hugged me as if I were a long-lost friend. All of a sudden, every typewriter ceased, and all eyes stared at us. The silence was as deafening as the typing had been moments earlier. Taffara ushered me into his office, ordered coffee and goodies, and gave me his full attention.

It wasn't until sometime later that I realized my friend was indeed a top leader in the nation, and here I was, in my missionary travel clothes, sitting, drinking coffee, and chatting with this great man. That day I got to know not only a great leader but also a humble man who had almost singlehandedly brought his country from poverty and famine to a place where his future dreams could have changed all of Ethiopia. Taffara had drawn up plans to build a dam that could be vital to the economic success of his beloved country. I could see why his vision was essential for water control and electricity, but this dream would require a stable government, and that was not to be.

Our conversation finally ended. Just before I left, Taffara said, "Take my card. If you have any problems, show the people my name card; maybe it will help you." I thanked him, tucked it in my purse, and headed back to the mission station.

As I waited for the bus, there were many people pressing in around me. I tried to strike up a conversation with some of them, but my Amharic and their English left much to be desired. Finally, a young man boldly pushed his way toward me and demanded to know what I was doing in his city. I told him I'd just come from a visit with Taffara DeGuefe.

"You couldn't have," he said belligerently.

Suddenly, I remembered the card I had just received. I took it from my purse and handed it to my college-aged challenger. Several onlookers crowded around us so that they could also see the card. The entire crowd suddenly backed away, apologizing as they made a way for me to get on the bus. I marveled at the power of this meek man's authority and popularity; merely showing his card changed everything.

Over the years, I've clearly seen the power of another name. It's the name I carry in my heart. Only *His* name is above all names. I was and still am awed by that name at which "…every knee should bow, in heaven and on earth and under the earth, and every tongue confess that Jesus Christ is Lord, to the glory of God the Father" (Phil. 2:10–11 NIV). "The name of the Lord is a strong tower," it says in Proverbs 18:10 (NASB); "the righteous runs into it and is safe." Taffara's name could save me for a brief moment in East Africa, but Jesus's name is what I depend on for all eternity.

Three days later, BBC came back on the air in Addis Ababa, announcing the coup and stating that all foreigners who wanted to leave could go the following day. The mission administrator, who had become a dear friend, offered to take me to the airport. She couldn't come into the airport to see me off, but I learned later that she sat in her little Volkswagen and waited until she saw my plane was safely in the air. She was concerned that the officials would change their minds, and she wanted to be sure I was really on my way to Israel.

For whosoever shall call upon the name of the Lord
shall be saved.

—ROMANS 10:13

14

LESSONS ON LEANING

THE SOLID ROCK IN POULSBO

AFTER MY FIRST world trip in 1974, I returned to complete my promise to give back two years to teaching before beginning my new career. I now knew I was to go, even if I wasn't sure where. I took great comfort in Hebrews 11:8, which says that Abraham went out, not knowing where he was going. I was not the first one in history to do something that looked foolish as I followed the word of the Lord.

Shortly after the Lord called me into full-time ministry, I was able to sell my five-bedroom, three-bath home. Some would say I gave it away, but I knew better: God showed me what to do, and I obeyed. A wonderful Christian family with five kids bought it, moved in, and touched the neighbors in ways I never could. The house I had boasted of when I was a child was a great blessing, but it was time to move on to the next phase of my life.

A few weeks before the house sale went through, I was teaching Bible in the town of Poulsbo, Washington. As I left this charming town on the Olympic Peninsula, the mountains showed their splendor, and it was breathtaking. I said to the Lord, "It would be wonderful to live in this beautiful town, Lord. Would you make that possible?" I was in the process of transitioning out of my comfortable life as a career schoolteacher and homeowner to walking by faith in full-time ministry. I wondered what my next step should be as I left my house and predictable paycheck.

Not more than two weeks later, I received a letter from a couple in Poulsbo inviting me to come and live rent-free in their basement apartment. Immediately, I remembered asking the Lord if he would make a way for me to live in Poulsbo. This was not just a way; this was like a paved highway! What a precious Lord! My heart sang as I gratefully accepted their invitation.

Days later, I received another letter, this time from the British missionary I'd met in Kenya. I had invited Helen to come to the United States if she ever wanted a vacation. Now here she was asking if she could take me up on the offer. I wrote back and told her I had sold my home and was moving to an apartment in a charming town about an hour away. I would check with the owners and see if Helen could join me in the new surroundings. My Poulsbo friends quickly approved, and before I knew it, there were two of us sharing that one-bedroom apartment.

Helen saw I was on the road a lot, but she was glad to come along. I had no idea how much I needed a companion and coworker as I started this new venture. Helen was talented; she played guitar well and was a good worship leader. Folks loved her English accent and rich stories. She was looking for a change after twenty years of teaching in that private high school near Nairobi. We soon became a team; she helped me in my ministry in many different ways and was a real friend and companion.

Her month-long stay quickly passed, and Helen's visa was drawing to a close. We discussed my need for her gifts, and she felt she'd like to stay longer in America. Off we went to the immigration office in Seattle to ask for an extension for her visa.

Parking in downtown Seattle was a nightmare; it seemed like everyone was trying to get a visa that morning. I had no idea what a problem we were facing, so with literally no place to park, I pulled into a fifteen-minute parking space.

We dashed upstairs into the Office of Immigration. There we were, among a sea of Asian faces, all waiting to see one clerk. I sat down and realized it could take us a week to work through the line. Sitting there, I became aware of a very cranky employee trying to deal with all the waiting persons. As I watched her, I realized she was saying no to everyone who approached her. She had a reason to turn down every person she encountered. I checked the number of the persons being helped; there were fifteen in front of Helen and me. I began to pray earnestly; this woman didn't want to help anyone, and our number was coming up fast. "Oh, Father," I prayed, "we need favor, please!"

Luke 2:52 talks of Jesus increasing in favor with God and man. Favor means it is something that is not earned; it's just something you ask for if God would like to give it to you. Favor can make people respond positively to you even if they have no reason to. It can make a lot of difference when you are dealing with officials who can make your life difficult.

As the number fifteen turned over and we were called to the counter, another clerk came out of the back room and said, "I'll help the next person." The new worker smiled at us; what a change from the other clerk's body language and voice. I was so relieved I could hardly tell the new clerk about the need for an extension on Helen's visa.

After we explained our situation, the clerk said, "I'm not sure who can help you." She thought for a second and then turned to us and said, "Come with me." We walked behind the counter to join her as she went to an office where a very overworked man sat. He looked almost buried by piles of forms—boxes full, all needing attention. The poor man didn't seem to mind as our clerk explained the dilemma. He said, "Let's see if there is a way." He rocked back in his chair and pulled out a huge book of regulations. He opened to a certain page, nodded to himself, and said, "If another religious group can come in here and get extensions for religious work, why can't you?" He underlined the paragraph he had just read. "There, you see, I can give you a year's extension." He promptly wrote out a form, stamped it, smiled, and handed it to us.

We were so full of praise and thanks to God that I can't honestly say what we told the officer. We dashed back to our car, hoping it had not been towed, but the meter said we had one minute left. Then we really started a praise-and-worship session. We thanked our Father, who so obviously intervened in our need, and did it within fifteen minutes!

To the best of my recollection, that was the first time I asked for Father's favor, and it certainly wasn't the last.

Poulsbo had a long stretch of waterfront park that overlooked the fantastic Olympic Mountains. Helen and I often hiked to the water's edge. The city made a boardwalk over the water that was truly beautiful, and we enjoyed relaxing in that serene place.

One day, we watched in horror as big gravel trucks and backhoes tore up the grass and made a real mess of that property. Each day was worse than the day before as concrete, gravel, and mortar added to the unsightly view. I was really unhappy; why would anyone want to block the view of those glorious mountains? I love progress of all kinds and will even drive out of my way to look at building projects in process, but this was ugly. What were they thinking?

Finally, one morning a huge truck came to the place where all the construction was taking place. On the truck flatbed lay a mammoth rock, easily ten to fifteen feet high and wide. The workers placed the rock in the middle of the gravel and proceeded to cement it into place. Now I was sure they had blocked that expansive view of Puget Sound and the Olympics. I was irked and said so repeatedly. It didn't seem to bother Helen, but I was perturbed; they ruined my favorite place.

One night soon after, I had a dream. In my dream, there was that ugly old rock. In my sleep, I heard the Lord speak to me.

You don't like that rock, do you?

I agreed. I hated it.

He said, *Go down, and lean against that rock.*

In my dream, I obeyed. I walked up to the rock, turned around, and let the rock hold my weight. As I felt the rock take all the weight and pressures off my body, the Voice spoke again. I saw daisies all around the rock—big Shasta daisies, my favorite flower, were everywhere.

Jesus seemed to say, *Now, go sit on the daisies.*

My response was, "No, Lord, I will crush the beautiful flowers."

The Lord answered, saying that was true. He continued by gently telling me those flowers represented the gifts of friendships He provided for me. *They will remain beautiful as long as you don't go and sit on them,* He gently told me. *I am that Rock you are leaning on. If you'll come to Me and lean on Me, I will take your burdens and hurts. Lean on me, Esther. I am strong, and I will meet all your needs. I have provided the daisies as friends and companions, but I want you to lean on Me. Then you will never crush the daisies.*

I woke up the next morning very aware of my nighttime conversation with the Lord. I couldn't wait to go check out that rock in real life. As soon as I could, I went down to the waterfront, eager for a close look. I knew there were no daisies around it in real life, but I wanted to see if there really was a place that would fit me like it did in my dream. I walked up to the rock to the same place I was in the night and leaned in. Sure enough, all the weight of my body was held by the rock. I was so touched that the God of the universe took time to teach me that lesson.

Several days later, I taught a Bible study at a church in nearby Silverdale. I couldn't wait to share with the ladies what I learned about leaning on the rock and not crushing the daisies. As I finished the study, the ladies rose as one. "We're going to the rock!" they announced. "We have to see if there's a place for each of us!" Car after car drove down the road to the Poulsbo waterfront. Each woman found her own special place and leaned into the rock.

I was no longer angry with the city for ruining my view. Instead, they gave me a way to get to know Father even better. And they saved me from crushing some of my own daisies along the way.

> The LORD is my rock, and my fortress, and my deliverer; my God, my strength, in whom I will trust; my buckler, and the horn of my salvation, and my high tower. I will call upon the LORD, who is worthy to be praised.
>
> —PSALM 18:2–3A

15

FAITHFUL FATHER

POULSBO POST OFFICE

ALL MY LIFE, I have noticed spiritual leaders seemed to be in financial need. As a child of God, I was always aware of their needs. Why did missionaries have to plead their cases in church after church to receive paltry offerings? I wondered.

Giving, however, was modeled from my youth. As a young child during the Depression, I watched Dad faithfully put money into the offering plate at church. In fact, sometimes his dollar bill was the only money in the plate. One day, I remember him saying to my brother, "You'll never have enough unless you start giving to God what belongs to Him." I watched that lesson unfold over the years, as my brother often had to borrow from others. He wasn't wasteful and worked very hard for his money, but he was not living a life of blessing. In his final days, that same brother often asked me if I needed money and even asked me to find others who had a need so he could help. At last, near the end of his life, his provision was blessed, and he was able to be generous.

When the time came for me to begin to think about my future expenses as a missionary walking by faith, I turned to my faithful heavenly Father. As I look back on that prayer, I am always amazed how He continues to answer it. I said something like this: "Father, it has always bothered me the way Your ministers have to ask, even beg at times, and worry about their needs being met. I don't want to live that way, so I am asking today if You will provide for me. I do not want to ask or tell anyone what my needs are. If You take care of me, I will try to be faithful to You."

Over the years, and especially in the early years, I had much to learn about trust. It began as I gave up my teaching job, sold my house, and received a monthly payment of $186.27 as I carried the mortgage. That house payment was the only guaranteed income I had. Still, I had a backup, I thought, as I was speaking at many Aglow International meetings, where I received offerings for my labor and I had been given a rent-free basement apartment to live in. Time went by, but I received no calls to minister, and I realized I was nearly broke. *Hmm*, I thought. When I was a schoolteacher, I couldn't fit all the speaking invitations into my schedule. Now I was available full time, and the phone was silent.

One day, when no calls to minister had come in, I was down to $103. I prayed harder for work, but still no speaking invitations came, and I was getting nervous. In my anxiety, I began to question my call. To my shock, the answer to my prayer was clear and instant: *Give me a love gift.* A love gift, when I was down to only $103?

I was at a loss—what should I do? I didn't know anyone I could ask for advice; no one else I knew was walking this crazy lifestyle, and it certainly didn't make any sense to my logical mind to give God a love gift when I had no promise of a paycheck and was nearly broke. Panic and fear tried to rule in my heart.

My temporary residence was on top of a high hill with the charming town of Poulsbo at the bottom. The only post office in town was down that long, long hill. I felt God was leading me to send a check to someone needy to show my love for Him. I argued with myself.

How much should I give? Finally, I wrote out a check for $50, walked down that hill, and quickly mailed it, trying to get the incident out of my mind while searching for the peace that follows obedience. Sadly, when I returned home, the ache in my heart was still there, and there was no peace. All along I'd known the Lord had asked me for $100, not $50. Partial obedience does not bring peace!

As I opened the door to my apartment, I knew I had to write the second check and mail my last $50 away. I reluctantly got the checkbook back out, wrote another check, and again walked down that long hill to the post office. This time, peace flooded my soul. My mind said, *If God doesn't come through now, I'm finished!* But peace was there, so I returned home with lighter steps.

When I opened the door to my apartment, I noticed something on my table. There was a $50 bill with no explanation, no name, nothing. I sat down and cried. Was Jesus really going to take care of my expenses? Was He really able to care for the details of my financial life? There were many more lessons to come. Still, God had been faithful, and I had not told anyone about my need. The next week, I shared my story of victory with my prayer group, not knowing that the next test was right around the corner.

A friend in the prayer group had connections with the school district, so she told them about a former PE teacher who would likely be available as a sub. In just a few days, my telephone rang. "Please help us; we desperately need a substitute teacher." I accepted the call and found myself right back where I had started this journey—in a public school classroom, teaching physical education.

Joy fled. When God called me out of teaching, He did not intend for me to look back. Substitute-teacher pay did not compare with the salary I left at the top of the pay scale. What was I doing? Would it help God if I earned a few dollars, or was God going to pay my way? Could I really count on Him?

The next day, I called the school district and asked that my name be removed from their substitute teacher list. I did not want to be like the apostle Peter; he spent three years with Jesus, but when times were tough and he didn't understand what was going on, he told the other disciples he wanted to go back to fishing (John 21:3). My battle was far from over, but I was slowly beginning to trust the Lord.

> Trust in the LORD with all your heart,
> And lean not on your own understanding;
> In all your ways acknowledge Him,
> And He shall direct your paths.

> —PROVERBS 3:5–6 (NKJV)

16

BELLEVUE PROFESSIONALS

S HORTLY AFTER MY substitute teacher "test," I received a phone invitation from Bellevue, Washington. There was a young-professionals group from different churches who wanted me to come and share at their Sunday school class in a nice restaurant's back room. This was a group of lawyers and doctors who were looking for someone to challenge them to know Jesus better, and I gladly accepted the invitation. My apartment was across the Olympic Peninsula from Seattle, so I either had to take a ferry over the water or drive around, taking the huge Tacoma Bridge to get around Puget Sound. Neither way was cheap, but I hoped to receive a decent love gift from these wealthy professionals, so I was not too concerned about my cost. Surely they would give me enough to cover my travel expenses. I found out I still had a lot to learn about God's ways with finances; He was not going to let people be my source of income, no matter how much money they made!

By 6:00 a.m. that Sunday morning, I was on the ferry. The sky was just coming to life. Summers in Washington State are breathtaking, and I really drank in the beauty. After driving through Seattle, taking the floating bridge across Lake Washington, making my way to Bellevue, and finding the restaurant, it was almost time to speak. It was indeed a large group of bright-looking professionals. I taught around thirty to thirty-five minutes and was blessed to see tears and other signs that told me people were being challenged to go deeper with Father.

Our meeting ended with lots of friendly sharing and good questions. Soon it was time for a quick closure, as everyone had to hurry back to their own churches for their Sunday-morning services.

I gathered up my materials, thanked my hostess for the love gift, and headed to the parking lot. When I opened the envelope to see how much I had been given, my heart sank. In it was my cash offering: a total of twelve dollars. Tears sprang to my eyes, followed by feelings of anger and not a little resentment. I called out to God and told Him my situation. Anger, tears—all the emotions came together as I blamed all those self-centered, rich young people and yes, God too. Why? Why? Wasn't I trying to please Him? Didn't He know how much I needed that money?

When I quieted down, I decided there weren't two options for the return trip. I had to go over the Tacoma Narrows Bridge to get home, as I didn't have the money for a ferry. I headed for I-5, full of frustration. The freeway near Kent, Washington, was only half a mile from the church I had attended before going into full-time ministry. Many good friends still attended there. Why not stop by church? It should be just starting.

I quickly pulled into the church parking lot, patted my tearstained face, and walked into the sanctuary. When the pastor saw me arrive, he announced to the congregation, "Esther has just come in!" It seemed like everyone turned to see me, with warm smiles of welcome. I was hardly ready to be greeted; all I really wanted was to be quiet and let my emotions heal. But God had other plans.

Pastor May stopped talking and said, "I believe God has just told me to take an offering for Esther." What a shock. The ushers scrambled, and plates were passed. When I left that service, Pastor handed me an envelope as he gave me a warm hug and assured me of their ongoing prayers. I returned to my car, put my Bible down on the seat, and opened the envelope. There was a check for $500. Once again the tears flowed, this time in shame. What kind of a God did I serve? He was so generous, and I was so undeserving.

I learned a song in childhood that told me that Jesus loved me when I was good, when I did the things I should. I did not qualify for this kindness with the attitude I had when I drove into the parking lot minutes earlier. Slowly, I was learning to *not* try to figure Him out but to trust Him and worship this tremendous friend I was just getting to know.

I can't even remember that trip home, but I do know I worshiped and sang and loved my Lord.

A few days later, I was reminded of a church camp going on in Oregon. That campground held special meaning for me, for it was there I first met Jesus as a thirteen-year-old. Friends had told me about a missionary speaker I knew in my younger years and later on in college. Trudy Hawley had gone to the Congo as a nurse, and many times our paths had crossed when she would return to Oregon for a much-needed rest. Now that I had gas money, I was off to Oregon to hear an update from Trudy about her work.

Trudy didn't tell me her very urgent need, but after three days, I learned from others that she had a medical appointment coming up in Portland. When I heard of her serious eye situation, I asked about the price of the medicine she needed. Reluctantly she told me the cost was $300. In the early 1970s, that was a huge financial mountain for any African missionary to climb.

I knew immediately that I had the solution. The offering Pastor May had so kindly taken for me had a call beyond my bank account—it was to help a Congo missionary get her eyesight back.

What a blessing to see tears in her eyes as I handed her the money she needed, and my heart danced with joy.

> And we know that all things work together for good
> to them that love God,
> to them who are the called according to his purpose.

—ROMANS 8:28

17

Go Ye into All the World

THE FIRST FEW months in my new career were exciting, challenging, lonely at times, and quite uncertain. I more than fulfilled my sabbatical requirements by returning to Cascade Junior High and teaching two years. Now fall had come, my new life was in full swing and winter was setting in. My apartment was cold, dark, and empty. Helen, my English friend who came from Africa and stayed many months to help with the ministry, had returned to England to live near her ailing parents. I felt that loss greatly; I even wondered if I was doing the Lord's will and began to question my call.

Sunday rolled around. I reluctantly got out of bed and thought maybe I'd watch a Christian program on TV. I wasn't really in the mood to get up and go to a church service and see a lot of people. I turned on the set, and to my amazement, the screen filled with a black-and-white sign. It said, "GO INTO ALL THE WORLD, AND PREACH THE GOSPEL." It was so commanding and startled me so much that I reached over, turned off the TV, and headed back to my bedroom to digest that message. The living room was cold, so I was hurrying toward my warm bed. Just then, my upstairs neighbor called down and said, "Esther, I have two of these maga-zines; would you like one? They're pretty good."

I said, "Sure, just toss it down the stairs. Thanks." The magazine landed face up, and on the cover it said, "GO INTO ALL THE WORLD, AND PREACH THE GOSPEL." What a shock. Twice in five minutes I'd received the same command.

That wakeup call gave me enough go-power to decide to go to church after all. I headed to Silverdale United Methodist Church with that command very much on my mind. As I entered the sanctu-ary, a dear friend came rushing over to greet me. Her opening remark was, "Es, are you all right? I've been up for hours praying for you, and the Lord gave me a message for you: *Go into all the world, and preach the gospel to every creature.*"

I was so overwhelmed by His kindness and encouragement that I have never wondered again about His call on my life.

Having Helen with me those months showed me I couldn't do the task alone—I needed a team partner. With her gone, I saw that music was my obvious weakness. I quietly went to the Lord and made this request: "Father, I need someone to become my partner in this mission you are sending me on. I have no idea who that might be. I do know she needs to be musical, and I'd love to have someone who will be fully involved in ministry and have a heart so after you that she will not be looking for a man to meet her needs. Also, I need a person who knows how to pray."

God heard that prayer and, in His own wonderful way, answered it through a church leader from Seattle I had yet to meet.

PART 2
LIFE IN CANADA AND BEYOND

18

A Ministry Partner

Meeting Sharon

About a year passed. The Spirit of God was opening up several places for me to teach, but I did not enjoy those long drives alone back and forth from the Olympic Peninsula.

One time, I had just returned to Washington, where I was living with a friend. She acted as my secretary when I was unavailable and took a call from a church in Seattle asking if I'd speak at a women's retreat in three weeks. I wanted to say no, but the retreat center was just eight miles from where I was staying, and the ladies didn't mind if I went home at night to my own bed. So, with the assurance that it was nearby and that my own bed was my reward, I accepted the invitation. I didn't know that God also had a plan for me at that retreat that would change my ministry and answer some private requests I'd been making. It's hard to learn that God often moves in what we consider inconvenience.

It was very dark, cold, and wet at that isolated campground when I arrived for the retreat, and I couldn't find a soul. After several stops and inquiries as to where the camp was located and then not finding anyone there, I was getting a little impatient. I prayed, waited, then decided I'd just go back home. But there was one building with a small patch of light in a large pavilion. I tried the door and found it open, only to find that little glow I had seen was coming from a tiny fire in a very large fireplace. There in the dark was one young woman, valiantly trying to ward off the cold and darkness with a few pieces of wood. Her name was Karen, and she assured me that yes, we were in the right place, and no, the bus bringing all the other ladies was due but had not yet arrived. I went back to my car to try to warm up and wait for her friends.

Ninety long minutes later, the bus finally arrived. The two-and-a-half-hour trip had turned into a four-hour journey, thanks to a flat tire along the way. There were many reasons that bus was nicknamed Job! Off came a gang of noisy, excited women, away for a weekend and hardly aware of the evening passing away. As the ladies went to choose their sleeping quarters, a tall young woman introduced herself and asked if I would like a couple of songs before I began to teach. I answered in crisp tones. "I think we've waited long enough, don't you?" She seemed to take my rudeness in stride; I was ready to get this show on the road! I did not have a clue I had just met God's answer to my prayers for a ministry partner.

Finally, all the rooms had been chosen, beds made up, and junk stuffed on every chair. It was a crazy mixture of scarves, jackets, slippers, boots, and Bibles as the ladies chattered their way into the meeting room. I was too grouchy to be impressed and was probably the only one in the whole camp that was not all that excited about the coming weekend. I am a real morning person, and this first meeting was starting close to my bed time.

God had laid it on my heart to share a study from Joshua. I called it "The Making of a Leader." From that not-too-smooth beginning, the weekend progressed into a beautiful time together in the Word. I began to realize this worship leader named Sharon had a real talent for bringing the ladies into God's presence. I also felt ministered to when she played the piano. To this day, once I am brought into God's presence through worship music, He faithfully rebuilds my spirit and even gives me energy. I thanked Sharon for her ministry and hugged all the ladies good-bye.

Later that fall, I was again invited to speak for Aglow International and several churches. Invitations kept coming from Victoria, it seemed. My practice was to invite a woman friend to go with me. I was walking down the steep hill near where I lived, praying about the next trip, asking God who I should take along. *Sharon*, I thought He said. I couldn't think of any Sharon, but then the Lord brought her face to mind. I didn't even remember her last name, but my friend and secretary did. I had enjoyed Sharon's skill and humble heart at the retreat and was tired of the solo commute to Victoria, so I invited her along after the Holy Spirit's prompting.

We got acquainted as we drove north on I-5; we were both serving the Lord but in very different ways. After she helped me at a couple of the church meetings in Victoria, I realized again how much easier it was to watch the Holy Spirit stir hearts and prepare folks for worship with her help. I said, "Boy, I could really use someone like you in my ministry—someone to lead in worship and help talk with the people."

"You have your ministry," she said, smiling, "and I have mine."

That was the end of the conversation, so I didn't give it another thought. I really hadn't meant it as a job offer but more like a compliment. She had a very effective ministry in her church, and I meant the compliment, even if I didn't think of it again.

But God was at work behind the scenes. That night, still in Victoria, we were staying in my good friends' home. I slept peacefully upstairs, while Sharon was tucked into the little sewing room hide-a-bed on the main floor. As she was reading Psalm 91, and before closing her eyes, the Lord spoke to her spirit. *You asked me for more faith. Were you serious?* His question took her by surprise. In her mind's eye, He showed her exactly where she was when she prayed that prayer. She was sitting in her church office, preparing for seventh- and eighth-grade confirmation classes. Sharon had no words of reply. Then, a second question came to her heart. *Are you willing to give up the security you have in Seattle?* That gave her great pause. Sharon sat in her little hide-a-bed with her Bible on her lap and thought about her life. She was content, and things were going well—she had no complaints, so she started to cry. God's gentle, gentle voice spoke to her heart a third time. *Don't you know that any time I have ever asked you to give up anything for me, I have always returned it to you a hundredfold?* She thought over her past years. It was true—each time she had followed God, the results were far better than her life before. That settled it. She knew she was supposed to leave her job and comfortable life in Seattle and join me in the unpredictable walk of faith to parts unknown.

I, however, knew nothing about this divine conversation. I totally forgot about giving Sharon an invitation to join me in my ministry— I was just trying to encourage her. Little did I know, God was going to use that offhand comment to change not only her life but mine. She told me about her conversation with God, but she didn't realize it was pretty common for women to approach me and tell me something similar. I tried to put her off by saying if that was God, wouldn't He tell me first? That made sense to both of us, but that was not what He chose to do this time.

We originally met in September and ministered together in October. We got a little more acquainted when I would pass through Seattle in the next months. The following February, my daily readings took me to 1 and 2 Kings. As I looked at the story of Elijah and Elisha, things started to make sense to me. I had asked God for a ministry partner, and here she was.

I moved to Victoria in February of 1979, and Sharon joined me in June. We accepted invitations to be a part of a nondenominational Bible school called Vancouver Island Christian Village. Friends found us a little apartment in charming Oak Bay that was not far from where the classes were held.

By the fall of 1979, Sharon had met all my family, and I had met all of hers. We took off for a trip around the world—my follow-up visit to some of the places I visited five years earlier, when God was my only companion. We often laugh about Sharon vomiting her way around the world and losing twenty-two pounds while I seemed to gain them! Along the way, though, we found many folks to minister to. In time, God spoke to her heart as well about a call to the nations. He told her He had given her an American passport but was calling her to the whole world.

For the next twenty-five years, we returned almost every year to Southeast Asia as well as other countries as God led. We ministered at retreats, listened to many people, prayed for many concerns, and learned more and more about tough mission calls.

Declare His glory among the nations, His wonders
among all peoples.

—Psalm 96:3 (NKJV)

19

FLOWERS, FLOWERS, AND MORE FLOWERS

M ANY YEARS AGO, before my spiritual-care ministry began, my desire to grow things and create my own world of beauty urged me toward wanting my own home. Eventually, I was led to that big house I wrote about earlier that was partly finished with a totally undeveloped yard. It was at this home that I began to love working outside. I built fences and put in underground sprinklers and light systems, loving every minute of it. Working on the landscaping filled much of my free time. Flowers, blue spruce, noble firs, and even giant cedars soon filled my yard and rose garden, separating my home from my neighbors' houses.

Now I had left all that creating and building behind and found myself back in an apartment in Victoria. There are many beautiful gardens in that city; at that time, most of the homes around Sharon and me were modest, but everyone worked hard to have beautiful flowers. At our third-floor apartment, however, there was no room for flowers. Our narrow little balcony faced east, but buildings and trees kept it protected from much-needed sunlight. Add to that British Columbia's long rainy seasons and very gray skies, and I was a discouraged gardener.

One day, my inner self felt very pent up, and I started complaining to my Father. "I need space, land, flowers, and a change," I griped to Him. I wasn't nice in my outburst. "Father, can't You give me someplace to grow flowers? I'm tired of looking at buildings and cars." Later, I remembered I hadn't moved to Canada to plant gardens. I did feel badly about spouting off to God, but I don't remember repenting.

It wasn't long after that our doorbell rang, and there stood our pastor with his arms full of flowers. He was quite a sight in his clerical shirt and collar, khaki shorts, long black knee socks, and sandals. We could barely see his head through the huge bouquet.

"Hi!" he said warmly. "I just came from a funeral service, and the family sent me off with all these flowers. I was wondering if you would like to have them."

Sharon and I were stunned. Neil hadn't heard my outburst, but God had. We couldn't believe God could and would answer so quickly!

Those were the first flowers God sent us after I complained, and each week as one flower bouquet began to die, there came another. One was lovely roses from a friend who thought we'd like the colors. On and on flowers appeared, often overlapping, though we never told anyone about our ongoing miracle.

The flowers were still coming when we were walking one day through Victoria's beautiful Beacon Hill Park. As we walked, we noticed a gardener pulling out dahlias from the flower beds. Now, dahlias just happened to be one of my favorite flowers, so we asked what he was doing as he made huge piles of flowers that were still in bloom.

"We have to make room for our new plants, so these have to go. Would you like some?" he asked.

"Yes, we would love to have some of your beautiful flowers," we said.

"Take all you want," he told us. It was like turning kids loose in a candy store! We dashed to the parking lot and brought the car nearer, and then we opened the large trunk of my Pontiac and filled the entire thing. We hurried home, where we filled the bathtub with our treasures. Then we became like the lady in 2 Kings 4, who sent her children out to collect as many vessels as they could find. We made flower arrangements in all kinds of holders for everyone we could think of, sharing our bounty.

By late fall, the flowers were still coming and kept appearing until we left for our winter season in Asia, where flowers grew on trees and orchids were twenty-five cents a stem. Still, we remembered with deep gratitude the tender love gift Father provided to His frustrated gardener. A few years later, He moved us to a small farm, where we were surrounded by gardens and flowers. Sweet Home, Oregon followed, and now Idaho, so I have never lacked for a place to grow things again. Thank you, Father; what a wonderful God You are.

But seek first his kingdom and his righteousness,
and all these things will be given to you as well.

—Matthew 6:33 (NIV)

No good thing will he withhold from them who walk
uprightly.

—Psalm 84:11b

20

A Dream Apartment

MANY FOLKS ASK Sharon and me how in the world we provide for ourselves. I mentioned earlier about my request to Father for His way to support us. To His honor and glory, I will share a few of the times He so marvelously sent finances. Remember, we have been in this ministry for over thirty-five years.

We learned that by giving to others' needs at His leading, we were always cared for. But it does require faith. In the Kingdom of God, the rules for provision are based on God's character and faithfulness.

The early days of ministering together based in Victoria were pretty lean. We had no salary, so our support seemed to depend on how often I was asked to speak. Just paying the rent was a stretch. Things got worse, though, when dear Pastor Neil insisted on giving us some salary.

"You are helping us all the time," he insisted, "so we should pay you something." He wrote out a check to us for five hundred dollars, saying he would do that monthly. Immediately, all our other sources dried up. We finally had to return to him and tell him there was no way he could pay us—we were starving to death! He shook his head and told us he would never understand our lifestyle, but soon funds started to flow our direction again.

We began our ministry partnership in a tiny one-bedroom apartment and then moved down Oak Bay Avenue to a little bit larger basement apartment, still one bedroom. Our not-so-dear upstairs renter neighbor was noisy and liked late-night parties. Down the hall and around the corner was a renter who was such a grouch that Sharon dreaded even seeing her. Invariably, our laundry time overlapped with hers. If Sharon did anything differently than Mrs. Johnson would have done it, she was in for a tongue-lashing.

In the meantime, I needed a way to get my hands dirty. I craved some flowerbeds or something outside to do to keep me happy. When the apartment manager announced yet another rent increase, we decided it was time to look for a bigger apartment. We prayed and asked for help from our loving Father.

Our very special friend Joanne decided she should help us find a better place to live. Jo asked us to make a list of all the things we needed and a second list of all the things that would be a bonus in our next home. We had never done such a thing, but it sounded like fun, so we took her advice. Two bedrooms were high on the list for Sharon, and a place for growing things was the top of my list. Lots of light was important after our basement experience. A kitchen larger than a hallway would help, as we often shared meals with people. We put down that we would like either a fireplace or a view; as long as we were dreaming, why not make it big? We were weary of looking out at a parking lot. Of course, we wanted it to be quiet and safe.

Joanne cheerfully took our list and began her search. To our great surprise, she was back in just a few days.

"I found it!" she said joyfully. "I know you're just going to love it! It has everything on your list except a fireplace!"

We followed her over to the Gorge Waterway, a quiet place with hidden beauty. What a view met us as we stepped into the two-bedroom apartment. There was much more space, no street noise, and a panoramic view of water, tall fir trees, and parkland. The living room was full of light. It was a corner unit on the second floor with a welcoming single woman next door. To our delight, the complex also included a full swimming pool. Now for the big question: How much was the rent?

Sadly, it was almost twice as much as our little place in Oak Bay. I'm ashamed to say that I was the one who immediately answered that we couldn't possibly take it, as it was too expensive. Sharon said very little, but I could see her answer wasn't going to be like mine. When she finally spoke, she was thoughtful.

"Now, let me get this straight," she said. She was new at the faith walk, so was trying to understand the ways of God through me. "God can provide two hundred and fifty dollars a month, but five hundred dollars is too much?" That jolted me. I was thinking Sharon and I were supposed to provide the rent. Sharon was reminding me that if God provided in the past, why would He not do it in the future? Was God that poor, or did He really want to bless us?

Conviction raced through me. I quickly admitted my error, asked for forgiveness, and God graciously, faithfully paid our rent for the entire time we lived on that gorgeous waterway. Fortunately for us, our Father forgives and often surprises us with far greater blessings than we ever think possible. We hosted a women's retreat there and many home meetings; several pastors found respite in our little hideaway too. Joanne's search led to a place that not only filled our needs but blessed many others. And I learned that God was way bigger than I thought!

Ask, and it shall be given you; seek, and ye shall find;
knock, and it shall be opened unto you.

—MATTHEW 7:7

21

A WALL OF FIRE AROUND US

ANGELS WATCHING OVER US

MANILA WAS NEVER my favorite city to travel to, but many of our Christian friends worked there, and we needed to go and encourage them. It was one of my first stops on my original world tour. Many relationships began and doors opened, so it became a regular stop on our overseas trips. Through the years, I suppose we spent almost three years in the Philippines. We forged lasting friendships with many missionaries who worked there and found it easy to love the gentle Filipinos we met along the way.

One year, our assignment was to relieve a family who needed to return to the States. We were asked to fill in for Fos and his family, overseeing their work as we lived in their house above the ministry office. They had moved from Singapore where I met them on my first trip, and now were expanding their art ministry to include other outreaches.

There were about eight folks who worked in the lower part of our house. Their main job description was to send out correspondence Bible studies, which were follow-up requests to the ministry of Athletes in Action. College-aged basketball players from America came to the Philippines and played teams of nationals (Filipinos love basketball). At halftime, the tall, handsome foreigners would share their testimonies of meeting Jesus. They would pray with people and then get signups for a four-part Bible correspondence course on the book of John. Many people responded every game. When the requests were mailed in, our team would correct the Bible studies, return them to the new Bible students, and then send out the next Bible study. All we were to do was be helpers and encouragers to this faithful team of follow-up workers.

We lived upstairs in this big old house, and by 5:00 p.m. each evening, all the workers went home. Darkness fell at about 6:30 p.m. (there is no twilight in the tropics—it seems like God shuts off the light, and suddenly it is very dark). Our residence was next door to Open Doors ministry, a group of believers dedicated to getting Bibles to Christians in closed countries. We became quite good friends with the guard who was assigned to protect their gates.

Looting was continually a challenge, and burglary was pretty common. Armed guards were a normal part of life in Manila. Every bank had several of these guards, and even McDonald's employed gun-carrying, uniformed men.

Open Doors was surrounded by large cement walls, easily fifteen feet high. We wondered why a guard would need a rifle for protection. The gate into their property was made of heavy steel fencing, and the guard would sit behind those gates, peeking through a small hole to see who wanted to come in.

Our house sat back on the property and was quite a contrast to our neighbors' homes. Ours was an old, plantation-style wood-frame building, a leftover from World War II days. We had no fence across the front of our property, only a couple of wires down on the ground. We did have a weed-filled ditch about a foot wide and a gate that looked somewhat official. It opened so that we could drive Fos's car onto the property. We locked our gate in the evenings, often wondering why we bothered, as anyone could walk around the gatepost and be in the yard with no resistance.

An unusual feature of our home was that the large front room was made of screens on three sides. Three feet of wood were attached to the mahogany flooring—a wainscoting—but above that was open screening. The breezes it allowed were wonderful, but it brought serious privacy issues. At night, our every action in the front of the house could be observed by many neighbors who lived in small dwellings across the street, as there were no blinds to cover the windows. The only privacy was in the back of the house, where we cooked, ate, and slept.

The house lot had large, beautiful trees. There was no streetlight, so the area was very dark as we looked out and very clear to all who looked in. We were the neighborhood lighthouse! Every other home on our side of the street was behind high walls, with the wide wall tops studded with broken glass. Every other home had hired private guards. When we asked why so much protection was needed, we were told of a murder nearby and the general fear of break-ins. We had an earlier incident of a purse-snatching—a man flew by us on a motorcycle and grabbed my purse as we walked near our home—but all in all, we felt pretty safe there.

Once again, evening came, and our workers had all gone home. We faithfully locked our gate and retired for the night. When we got up the next morning, there was a stir in the neighborhood. We learned about it from our yardman, who got the full scoop from the people across the street. Apparently, a carload of drunken men had come by and tried to get into our gate. The five men banged and banged on our gate, trying to break the lock. Our neighbors watched in horror behind closed doors, fearful to see what would happen to the two white ladies. Suddenly, a streetlight flashed on. It startled the men and threw them off in their plan. The neighbors watched as the drunken men quickly jumped back into their car and fled.

Streetlight? What streetlight? It hadn't worked in five years, but that night it burned brightly, effectively terrifying the would-be thieves.

Humbly, we thanked our precious Savior for His protection. As we prayed, I could see in my mind's eye that even though our walls were not secure, we were safe. I saw two huge angels were on assignment, one on either side of the gate, watching over the house without walls. Our praying friends back home had us covered in ways no walls or wire could protect us, and our God kept us safe from harm. There were no other incidents during our stay there.

"And I myself will be a wall of fire around it,"
declares the LORD, "and I will be its glory within."

—ZECHARIAH 2:5 (NIV)

22

WHERE DID THAT BUS GO?

MANILA-BAGABAG TRIP

DICTIONARY.COM SAYS THAT a miracle is a "surprising and welcome event that is not explicable by natural or scientific laws and is therefore considered to be the work of a divine agency." Have you ever experienced a miracle that was truly undeniable? Most folks I talk to say they haven't personally experienced one, but Sharon and I have more than once.

It was my second trip to the Philippines and Sharon's first. I was introduced to Wycliffe Bible Translators and stayed in the Summer Institute of Linguistics Guest House on my first visit to Manila. It was a hub of missionary activity that offered inexpensive meals and lodging so that missionaries from distant places could meet and find fellowship while they accomplished their city errands and medical appointments. It was a guarded compound close to major thoroughfares and a great place for us to interact with various missionaries.

While staying there, we were invited to share with teachers' wives at Faith Academy near Manila and speak for other Christian outreaches in the area. Several Wycliffe missionaries mentioned we might want to see the work of Summer Institute of Linguistics at their center north of Manila, near a little town called Bagabag (Buh-GAH-bug). The center included a grade school for children of missionaries who lived at distant allocations, as well as support staff who were hungry for fellowship and fresh input. Bible translators had modest houses where they could come for a break from intense tribal living while they continued their work.

Philippine Airlines had discontinued their flights from Manila to Bagabag. By road it was a long and weary journey, averaging between six and eight hours each way. Most missionaries made the trip on rickety, well-worn buses. At the bus station, we met two S.I.L. workers who were also headed to Bagabag. Having new people to share the all-day, backbreaking, cramped-leg journey with made the trip seem shorter and more interesting.

Our crowded bus rattled out of Manila and onto a good highway heading north. Sharon turned around in the seat, chatting with the missionary ladies. I suggested we change seats so we could get better acquainted. Soon, Sharon was sitting behind me with one missionary lady while I chatted with my new seatmate.

At every small town, people piled on with their produce, groceries, large rice sacks, and even a few chickens. Along the way, I realized the bus driver was overly attentive to one of the more attractive young women on board. He was driving recklessly and obviously trying to impress her. She sat very near the back, but that didn't stop their ongoing flirtation.

Seldom on those narrow mountain roads did vehicles try to pass—there was very little space to maneuver. As the driver was busy giving his attention through the mirror to the young lady, who had casually moved closer to the front, we were suddenly in great danger. A big, more expensive bus roared up and quickly pulled out in front of us. I could see our driver did not like that, so he began to try to overtake the much larger and more powerful bus. His desire was obvious: he'd show that bus he also had power and impress his new lady friend.

By now, he was building up speed and pulled over the middle of the road to pass. Just then I looked up and saw a large truck cresting the hill, heading toward us. We were squarely in the truck's lane with nowhere to go. The green bean Voice inside me shouted, *Pray!* I turned to look at Sharon and yelled, "Pray!" I'm sure urgency filled my voice. All I could see was that the bus we were trying to pass was next to us on the narrow road, while the large truck stared down at us as he descended the hill. On our right was a mountainside, on our left a deep chasm. There was no way of escape.

Everything happened so fast I still cannot accurately relay the events. My eyes were closed tightly as I prayed and braced for a horrible accident in the middle of tropical isolation on a Philippine island.

Suddenly, we were past the bus. The truck was still on the road, headed toward Manila. Somehow—God only knows how—all three vehicles passed on a two-lane mountain road without a scratch.

Great fear shot like lightning through the bus as all of us realized we should be dead. Terrible quietness, shock, and then relief came as people began to chatter about our near disaster. The embarrassed young woman who had caused part of the problem returned as casually as she could to her seat at the rear of the bus. I knew God had made a path for us where there was no room for even a *person* to pass. We four missionary women knew without a doubt that God had spared our lives.

Before we left our work in Canada to go on this three-month trip, our friend Audrey had set up a twenty-four-hour prayer chain for us. At times, it felt like all those prayers were going into a huge kettle so that when a need arose, all we had to do was dip in. Were angels on assignment? I had no doubt. Were people praying for us back in

Canada and the United States? They must have been. We trembled all the way into Bagabag, praising God for his gracious gift of life.

> The effectual fervent prayer of a righteous man avai-
> leth much.
>
> —JAMES 5:16B

> Where can I go from your Spirit?
>
> —PSALM 139:7A (NIV)

> For he shall give his angels charge over thee, to keep
> thee in all thy ways.
>
> —PSALM 91:11

23

THE JUNIPER TREE

CHINESE NEW YEAR AND CENTRAL THAILAND

WHEN I WAS a freshman in college, my first dorm experience was much like a calf being set free from a pen—frisky and leaping for joy! I didn't think of my upbringing as strict; Dad and Allie trusted me, so I lived without many restrictions. I had a fierce love for my dad, having lost my mother at the age of four, so I didn't want to displease him. That protected me from trying a lot of foolish things in my teen years at home.

Life at Seattle Pacific College was quite different, though; in the early 1950s, the Free Methodist school had definite ideas of how nice young Christian ladies should look and behave. I, however, was full of nonsense and thought it was great to pull tricks on my fellow class-mates. It didn't take long before the dorm mother took notice as my roommate Fran and I collected all the toothbrushes from our dorm floor and left them in the hallway for everyone to try to locate their own. Then there was the time we brought a bucketful of small crabs from the beach to distribute to all the rooms while the girls were out for the evening. Soon, there were squeals up and down the halls as the girls thought there had been a giant spider invasion. We wore the poor dorm mom out, and before long she quit that job and made her way to Asia as a missionary. Surely life in Vietnam couldn't be harder than dealing with unruly college freshmen in America!

I did have a few pangs of conscience when Ruth Wilson left SPC. I had played my way through high school, so I was unprepared for the rigors of college studies. To combat that, I stopped by the small chapel every day, got down on my knees, and humbly asked for help. At least one of those times, I repented of my childish actions that brought such grief to Ruth. Those contrite prayers might be why I never forgot her.

Years later, I was visiting a dear friend's home when Ruth stopped by. She was as shocked to see me as I was to run into her. As I sat and listened to her stories, I realized she had her hands full and needed much help. In the decades that had passed since we'd been thrown together at Seattle Pacific, I had quit my teaching job and was trying to be God's ambassador to the nations. She, meanwhile, was forced to leave Vietnam because of the war and courageously set up a home where weary missionaries could come away and rest. God gave her a beach house on the Gulf of Siam in South Thailand. Sharon and I listened to Ruth's heart as she told us she was able to keep a roof over their heads and food on the table for the tired Christian workers, but there was no time left to meet their spiritual needs. She recognized that it wasn't enough to just give them a beautiful location with a well-equipped library; these people needed spiritual care from other believers. Would we come and teach, renew, and challenge her many worn-out fellow workers? We learned that folks were coming to her getaway from all over Southeast Asia and China. Would we come and see if this was where God wanted us to serve?

How could we say no? She even handed me a twenty-baht bank note with instructions on how to get to the south bus terminal from the Bangkok airport, hoping that we'd take her up on her earnest plea.

We did indeed go in 1980, and that trip opened up the real purpose God had prepared for us for the next twenty-plus years. Friends from North America supported us by sending prayer, money, magazines, and current bestsellers. Several even accompanied us in our mission to help bridge the ocean with encouragement to His workers in the outback of Asia.

Each year in the lunar calendar, Chinese New Year is celebrated in January or February. Many Asians mark the holiday with false worship, traditions, hopes, and superstitions as they look ahead to a prosperous new year. It is a time when China's schools close, and therefore many foreign workers (often known as "Ms"—we think of them as missionaries), leave their guest countries and come out for a much-needed change and rest. Westerners living in Tibet, China, Bhutan, Mongolia, and other remote locations throughout Asia get on trains and start heading south to much warmer climates. We heard stories of people who started with five layers of clothing on to protect themselves from temperatures that hovered around fifty degrees Fahrenheit in their apartments. As they traveled south, layer after layer would be peeled off until they were ready for the white-sand beaches of Thailand and saltwater that was like a soothing bath.

The Westerners (most were American, with a smattering of Canadians and a few Europeans) came in droves to meet others, thaw out, work on business challenges, and get medical needs cared for. We would greet the weary travelers, help them learn the ropes around The Juniper Tree and our small fishing village, and offer almost-nightly meetings for their spiritual refreshment. Every evening, about 6:15 p.m., the sun would start to set; by 6:30 p.m. it was so dark you could barely see to walk on the beach. In the 1980s, Thailand was not yet a world-class destination for travelers, so The Juniper Tree, just past the small village of Huahin, was a quiet reprieve from bustling Asian cities of many thousands or millions. In later years, a fun night bazaar developed, copying the large, popular Night Market in

Chiangmai, Thailand, but in those early years, there were few options for entertainment after dark.

We began to hear tales of long months without fellowship or friends. Church services as we know them in the West were nonexistent in those faraway cities. People would weep as they joined in corporate worship, singing the latest scripture choruses while Sharon played the small keyboard we brought along. I would ask the Lord for a fresh word for His weary sheep, and He would faithfully make the scriptures come alive so His children could have some new spiritual food.

Often, Valentine's Day occurred during Chinese New Year. We always brought a party in our suitcases—chocolate, drink mixes, magazines, new Christian books, small prizes, new card games—anything to help people unwind. We would host a party with funny games and contests, serve chocolate-chip cookies (only North America had chocolate chips back then), and generally love the weary pilgrims. Their lives were full of giving; our job was to try for that brief time to give back to them.

As Huahin became a more popular destination, options grew. Some American fast-food restaurants started to appear, the Night Market was drawing crowds, and the little town developed a nightlife. We decided we could take a break one night a week so the folks could enjoy the town's features. One couple, however, didn't make the half-mile walk back into town to take advantage of the Night Market. When we asked them why, they told us tearfully that they had been listening to the same teaching cassette every Sunday for months, so they had stayed back, hoping there might be some kind of spiritual gathering after all. Their deep hunger challenged us, but we needed a break too. We were headed down the beach, about a half-hour walk away from town, to find a restaurant we were told had cheesecake with blueberries—unheard of in those parts. We asked them to join us and then paid for their desserts. They wept at the kind act. I don't remember canceling another meeting after that.

Gathering so many of God's workers led to invitations to come visit them on their home territory. We were invited to Laos, Cambodia, China, Nepal, Vietnam, other parts of Thailand, and even Kabul, Afghanistan. We prayed over each invitation and tried to follow God's leading. We were led to visit two German nurses who worked in the outback of Nepal. Another invitation took us to visit a couple working in North-Central Thailand. Thailand is roughly the size of Texas, with many trains and some air-conditioned buses easing the long miles between destinations. Now, of course, the trains are supplemented by superhighways and air travel, but then train travel was the primary way of getting around.

Our friends warmly welcomed us, and we were delighted to have time with them, but we had never been so hot. When we went to our second-floor bedroom to rest, the sheets felt like they had just been taken from a clothes dryer back home. The couple admitted to us that often they resorted to sleeping on the cement floor at the ground level, rolled up in sheets that had been dampened with cold water. As the water evaporated, that provided some cooling. We offered to take them out to eat; there was one restaurant in town with air conditioning, and it was beyond their budget.

Their ministry was to distribute gospel tracts and Bibles on a small scooter, so night and day there was no reprieve from the heat for them. Our immediate prayer on their behalf was, "Father, *please* give our friends a car so they can have some way to cool off!" We asked that it be big enough to carry all the books they were trying to distribute. This was our request, not theirs, as they were living very carefully on small missionary salaries, fully aware there was no way they could afford that kind of transportation. We assured the couple that God was not limited to their means, their mission's means, or even their friends' gifts—our job was to ask and trust, and God's job was to answer.

The following year, we were spending a few days at the Christian and Missionary Alliance guesthouse in Bangkok when in drove a couple in a beautiful, sky-blue van. Out of the passenger door bounded our friend. She ran over to where we were, leaped into my arms, and said, "He did it! God did it! He answered our prayers, and look what He gave us!" Her quiet husband came and joined in the hug-fest, and we were able to rejoice with them that our God, who knew their needs so well, brought them the impossible: a vehicle that was perfect for their work and exceedingly above all that they could ask or imagine (Eph. 3:20).

James 4:2 (NIV) says in part, "You do not have, because you do not ask God." Our friends were willing to do without air conditioning, but it seemed to us that they could be more effective in their work if they could have better transportation and a place where they could cool down. When we ask God for things that seem to be extravagant by some people's standards, we always give Him permission to say no. We trust our loving Father, but we also do not want to be guilty of not asking when there are blessings available. We asked, our friends were blessed, and we all rejoiced!

> O give thanks unto the LORD; for he is good: for his
> mercy endureth for ever.
>
> —PSALM 136:1

24

MORE THAN ENOUGH

FOOD MULTIPLYING

Ruth Wilson worked hard to care for her weary guests at The Juniper Tree. Running a missionary guesthouse is a full-time job, even if you have a great staff. Ruth toiled on day in and day out, so one year in the early '80s, we urged her to take advantage of our being there and head to Bangkok for a few days. She needed a run for supplies anyway, so when there appeared to be an opening with very few people booked, she decided to take us up on our offer. She planned to be gone just four days; what could go wrong in that short time?

We waved good-bye to her and enjoyed half an hour of peace before the first challenge came. Not knowing the water pipes were just below the surface, a guest drove his car under a tree and broke a pipe. Water gushed up while we rushed to find the shut-off valve. By God's grace, one of the visiting missionaries had some plumbing expertise. He quickly went to work, and the first emergency passed.

At 10:00 a.m., the phone rang. Four surprise walk-ins had just filled the last vacancies, so we were at capacity, but no one else was expected. Telephones were still pretty rare at that time in Thailand; if you wanted to make sure you communicated with someone, the best idea was to go to the post office, stand in line, and send a telegram. Guests from out of country weren't aware of that, so they would try to call. Sharon picked up the phone and struggled to make herself heard. A pleasant-sounding man was on the other end in Bangkok, though he sounded like he was across the ocean. With his heavy European accent, he told her he and three others were at the train station and planned to be at The Juniper Tree at 4:00 p.m. Could they please have two rooms and join us for the evening meal?

"I'm sorry," Sharon shouted into the phone, "there isn't any room."

"I can't hear you," the Finnish man shouted back. "We will see you this afternoon."

"No!" Sharon tried again. "We are full up!"

"I can't hear you," the man yelled. "We will see you at 4:00 p.m. Thank you! Hallelujah!" That's the one word that needs no translation no matter what language you speak.

Sharon hung up the phone. What would we do with two European couples whose English was limited when we had no beds? At that time, there were no other guesthouses or moderate hotels that we could send them to. And then there was the food issue; there were also no restaurants we could recommend.

Praying as she walked toward the kitchen, the next challenge was before her. The head cook knew some English, but she was out of town. The second cook was about ready to have a baby; she didn't need any drama added to her life. Her English was very limited, so the sign language began.

Fish and chips and a picnic was the plan for the evening meal. *Great*, Sharon thought, *I'll just ask her to buy another fish.* She didn't realize the cook had been to the market long before breakfast, purchasing the fish she thought was just right for the expected guests. Plus, the cook didn't realize that eight people had been added to her evening meal roster.

"Fish," Sharon said, measuring out about eighteen inches with her hands.

"Fish," the cook countered, measuring out about a foot.

Knowing that included head and tail, Sharon tried again. "Fish," she said firmly, with the same distance between her hands.

"Fish," was the reply, the cook unchanging. The poor woman had the tired, sweaty look of a very pregnant mom, standing in the tropical heat, trying to get lunch ready while this crazy American was being unreasonable about a fish size that wasn't going to change. Sharon backed off but had no idea how there would be enough food for the picnic.

The hours flew by. The four delightful Finnish Pentecostals arrived as they said and headed joyfully out for a swim. I'm not sure how we accommodated them, but somehow adequate sleeping arrangements were found. There was still the fish issue, however. A Dutch missionary family vacationing with us tried to help; they said they would share their four burgers and come join us for the picnic. We weren't sure how adding four more people with their four hamburgers would help, but we were grateful for their encouragement.

One of the workers rang the bell to signal the evening meal; the guests had played hard and were eager to enjoy some good food. The cook brought out the fried fish on a nice platter, surrounded by french fries. The fish looked even smaller than we expected; that head and tail sure took a lot of space but wouldn't fill hungry missionaries. The people gathered around the table to pray, fill their plates, and head outside to enjoy the festive meal. Sharon and I tried to hide our nervousness behind our smiles.

Asking God to bless the food was not just a good habit before this meal. It was a serious plea from our hearts that only God heard under the common words of grace. "Oh, God, please do something!" was the unspoken prayer.

The meal began. People were in good spirits as they filled their plates while Sharon and I held back, sharing conversation with the guests. When everyone had stepped outside, we looked at the table. There were three burgers still there as well as more than half the fish. How could that be? We each took a small serving of fish and chips and joined the others. Many returned for seconds and seemed to eat their fill. There was still food on the table, so I invited them back for thirds.

When the meal finished, we looked at the leftovers. About a third of the fish remained! We had no explanation for that, unless the same God who fed the multitudes in Bible times was still at it. We didn't ever see the food multiply; we just couldn't finish it off. What a blessing!

All I have needed Thy hand hath provided;
Great is Thy Faithfulness, Lord unto me.
© 1923, renewed 1951, Hope Publishing Co., Carol
Stream, IL 60188

Don't worry about anything; instead,
pray about everything.
Tell God what you need, and thank him for all he
has done. Then you will experience God's peace,
which exceeds anything we can understand.
His peace will guard your hearts and
minds as you live in Christ Jesus.

—Philippians 4:6,7 (NLT)

25

MANORAM HOSPITAL, THAILAND

ONE OF THE invitations to minister that came out of our time at The Juniper Tree led us to a hospital just sixty miles outside Bangkok. We enjoyed the bus ride that took us north of the teeming city; however, it led to a desert of steaming, hot plains. We were welcomed by Adele, a lovely Swiss woman, whose husband was the hospital administrator. She directed us to the guesthouse, where Sharon and I each had a private room. Or almost private—there were previous occupants that had four feet. We called these small lizards "geckos;" the Thai word sounded like "CHEE-chack," imitating the sound the little reptiles made.

Sharon came to check out my room and sat at the end of my bed. I was fretting about the visitors, saying they might fall on me.

"Don't worry," Sharon said casually. "Don't you remember they told us they have little suction cups on their feet and stick to the ceiling? Besides, they're your friends—they eat mosquitoes." At that moment, one fell from the ceiling and landed right on Sharon's foot. Not known as an athlete, she made the kick of her life, sending that lizard to a new location far across the room. So much for her advice! The pigs that rooted in the shade underneath our building didn't make us nearly as uncomfortable as the geckos inside.

My college studies started in premed, so being in this Christian mission hospital atmosphere was a delight for me. We learned of a surgeon that was changing many lepers' lives by actually moving muscles and tendons. Dr. Grace Warren was her name; she'd studied under Dr. Paul Brand[1] in India and then traveled about with the miraculous knowledge he had given her that brought useless hands, feet, fingers, and toes back to life. Amazing Grace, as she was known, found physical therapist Jo (one of the few Americans working at Manoram Hospital) an eager student, so Grace had a partner in restoring life. Leprosy destroys nerve endings, so when the patients came in for rehabilitation, and Jo detected a greenish spot under the skin, she knew infection had come. Since leprosy destroyed nerves, pain was not a problem. Jo could almost do major surgery on the patients without anesthetic or even a special room. A kitchen scouring pad became a lifesaving surgical instrument in Jo's loving, capable hands. I loved watching every movement. With the combination of the heat and gore, though, Sharon quickly looked for other places to spend her time.

In Bible times, lepers were the outcasts of society. Even though Biblical leprosy was a different disease than the skin and nerve problem called by that name today, lepers remained outcasts. We were told that it was highly unlikely that we could catch leprosy—that we would need a predisposition to the disease as well as exposure. At that time, leprosy could not be cured, but it could be held at bay for just twenty-five dollars a year. That was a figure beyond the reach of most rural Thais, though. The possibility of being social outcasts

---

1 Paul Brand, MD, according to his obituary, was the pioneer of muscle-tendon-transplant operations in leprosy patients. He partnered with Philip Yancey to write five books about the human body, leprosy, and other spiritual topics. He retired in West Seattle; we were honored to meet him when he spoke at a Christian camp in Bellingham, Washington.

kept many of them living in denial, even as they began to lose feeling in their extremities, so by the time they came to the hospital, the disease had often stolen their ability to walk or use their hands naturally. The patients did amazing things with wooden boxes and sticks (their substitutes for walkers and canes) and accomplished a lot with nubbins that used to be fingers. A telltale sign was the bridges of their noses sinking in; by then, the world could see at a glance that the dreaded disease had them in its grip.

Manoram Hospital changed the lives of so many suffering people. The quiet medical servants of the Lord devised seven different ways to share the story of Jesus's love with the people who came for medical treatment. Since the lepers needed to come back regularly for outpatient care, they were exposed to the gospel over and over. Even though most of the patients were Buddhists who came from generations of Buddhism and lived in a culture where schoolchildren in public schools daily pledged their allegiance to Buddha, many were heard to say they were so grateful they had become infected with leprosy. Why? "I would never have met Jesus otherwise."

The most beautiful sound we heard while staying at Manoram was the singing at 6:30 a.m. The lepers hosted a prayer meeting every morning that started with a song of worship. The missionaries agreed that if they wanted a prayer answered, they would bring their requests to the leprous believers. Those meetings were holy ground. "Blessed are the meek, for they shall inherit the earth," Jesus said in Matthew 5:5. These dear ones had very little in worldly wealth, but oh, they were rich in spirit.

The devil was not happy with the goings-on at Manoram Hospital. Dr. Elly was a bright Dutch physician who worked there and became our friend. One day, she was riding her motor scooter down the highway near the hospital when she was hit by a bus. The details were vague, as the bus driver did not stop after the accident.

Sometime later, Dr. Elly was found along the side of the road. Her coworkers rushed her to the hospital; she remained in a Bangkok medical facility for an extended time. Elly lost one ear and part of her skull in that horrible incident. This brilliant doctor who spoke multiple languages could only remember her native tongue. How could she practice medicine in Thailand in a hospital that functioned in Thai and where the missionary common language was English, when she could only recall Dutch? The brain injuries she suffered meant life would never be the same; her medical degrees allowed her to sign off for AIDS patients and do in-home care in later years, but what a price she paid for her missionary service.

Dr. Elly wasn't the only one who paid a high price for the spiritual fruit gained in Central Thailand. We visited the medical work there several times. On one visit, our friend Adele looked vulnerable, so we asked what was wrong. She set aside time in her very full schedule as the wife of the head doctor and began to tell us a tragic story. That very day was the anniversary of the saddest day in Manoram history. It was the day that two vanloads of children from the mission met with a horrible end in a traffic accident about an hour away from the hospital compound. The carnage was unspeakable; Adele and her husband lost a beloved son, and almost every young child (except a few infants) from the missionary group had been killed. We wept as Adele recalled the story; she told how she stood at the scene of the accident, in the midst of the bodies of the dead children of her coworkers, as well as the lifeless body of her own son, and boldly declared that Satan was a loser. No matter how things appeared, Jesus was the victor. For months after, she told us, the whole compound was like a tomb with the voices of their beloved children silenced. We were the only ones at Manoram that day who did *not* know that horrible story. We saw God's great kindness in bringing us at that time so this mother could share with fresh listeners the day of her deepest loss.

Blessed be the God and Father of our Lord Jesus Christ, the Father of mercies and God of all comfort, who comforts us in all our tribulation, that we may be able to comfort those who are in any trouble, with the comfort with which we ourselves are comforted by God. For as the sufferings of Christ abound in us, so our consolation also abounds through Christ.

—2 Corinthians 1:3–5 (NKJV)

26

BANGKOK WITH LORRIE AND JOKE

1983

Bangkok was our first stop in Thailand; we planned to meet two missionaries coming from Bangladesh and India. We invited them to join us at The Juniper Tree for a much-needed rest and debriefing on their way home to Victoria. Lorrie and Joke (YOKE-uh, a Dutch nickname for Johanna) were Canadians and good friends from our Victoria connection. We met Joke when she was working as a youth and parish worker while we were helping her pastor build his congregation. Lorrie was Joke's friend, a fellow youth director; both of them had just cut their teeth on their first mission. Now they were headed home and agreed to stop in Thailand to visit us on the return trip. Lorrie was ready to spend the rest of her life in India; Joke wasn't sure she would ever leave Canada again—it had been a rough time in Bangladesh.

None of us knew Bangkok well. We rented a hotel room for the four of us not too far from the airport and, to our surprise, found it was about as sleazy as it could be. We gladly slipped out of our room early and began our almost five-hour bus trip south. By this time, Sharon and I had learned not to take the orange bus line—they weren't called Orange Crushes for nothing—which was slow, hot, and painfully crowded. Instead, we traveled to Huahin on the blue bus line, where air conditioning, stewardesses, and free cold drinks were the norm. The trip was long and uneventful, but at last we arrived with eager plans to swim and relax on the Gulf of Thailand. Our friends were bone weary, and our comfortable retreat center right on the water's edge was just the medicine we thought they needed.

Those were good, restful days as we learned some very sad stories of overseas work. We also saw that our Canadian friends were not quitters, so we made them an offer. Come with us on the rest of our trip, we told them; come experience Hong Kong and the Philippines before you make more decisions about your future. We were glad they said yes, as they were later to see that it would be in Manila where others would help them begin a new children's ministry.

Meanwhile, back in Thailand, there was little to do at The Juniper Tree once the sun set. Sharon and I were there to lead worship and Bible teaching for those who desired fellowship and Bible studies. Joke and Lorrie reveled in the opportunities to be in nature and have some spiritual food as well.

After several days, though, on our last night there, Lorrie began to feel like something was very wrong in her sinuses. She stayed back in her room one evening, which was so unlike her, while the three of us went on to the meeting. On our return, we realized Lorrie was indeed quite ill. What to do? We prayed and decided to wait till morning, when we would make our way back to Bangkok.

Early the next day, we started our bus trip back to the city. Lorrie was increasingly more ill, and her face started swelling. The sun was shining brightly in her bus window. She loved the heat, but it made the swelling in her face accelerate. We were all worried about her. What was going on?

Sitting in the front row of our bus was a Mennonite woman who was a doctor in India. Lorrie was in the row behind her. The doctor took one look at Lorrie and whispered to us to find her a doctor as soon as we could. She then told us of a small Christian hospital not far from the bus depot. When we arrived in the city, we found a taxi driver, but his English wasn't any better than our Thai. Still, God was in charge; in minutes he had us right in front of the hospital entrance, even as he shook his head wondering how that had happened.

The four of us hurried to the front of the hospital, not knowing the Lord had just brought us to the only hospital in the city that had a doctor working in the emergency department. The doctor was a lovely Thai woman who took one look at Lorrie, grabbed her, and dashed into an empty room. In the meantime, Joke had her own issues and nearly fainted in the hallway. In the end, they were both admitted with completely different symptoms. The doctor hurriedly lanced a boil in Lorrie's nose, the source of her head swelling like a basketball. Rehydration helped Joke a lot, but there was great fear that infection from the boil could go to Lorrie's brain and kill her. We heard a story of a Canadian man who had been in a Bangkok hospital for a year because of the same thing: a boil that caused encephalitis of the brain.

That night was very scary for Lorrie. In the middle of the night, they put her in an ambulance and took her across town for further tests to make sure they were doing the right thing. The other hospital confirmed that she was getting the proper care, so they sent our weary friend back to her first bed.

Meanwhile, Sharon and I were at a missionary guesthouse all the way across the city. We called as early as we were able to check on our friends and learned that Joke was ready for release, but the doctor thought Lorrie should stay there at least a week to make sure the infection disappeared. The hospital charged a hundred dollars a day, which doesn't sound like much today, but in the early '80s, that was a big wallop to young missionaries.

We grabbed a taxi so we could pick up Joke and visit Lorrie. What could we do to minister to Lorrie? we wondered. Lord Jesus, what should we do? Sharon said, "I think we are supposed to take her communion." That sounded good, but where would we find bread and grape juice? We'd never seen grape juice in Thailand. We stopped by an international hotel on the way, where the gift shop sold small bottles of wine; that would do just fine.

When we entered Lorrie's room, we were shocked to see her eyes swollen shut and her small, thin face completely round. This was far worse than we expected; no wonder the hospital was monitoring her closely. We told her we brought communion, and without delay, all four of us shared the body and blood of Christ together. We knew only Jesus could heal Lorrie, and we were sincerely asking.

The next morning, we called Lorrie to check with her. To our amazement and God's glory, healing really began in the night. Lorrie still looked terrible, but her eyes were trying to open. The danger was past, and the doctor said we could take her to our guesthouse if we could provide a nurse to administer meds and give her shots. What a joy! We knew two German nurses vacationing from Nepal who would be glad to help with that. Lorrie's hospital stay went from a predicted weeklong stay to just two nights. Before that third day was over, Lorrie was in her room at the Alliance Guest Home and on her way to recovery.

We held an impromptu prayer-and-praise session when we got Lorrie home. Just four short days later, we were able to carry on with our journey to Hong Kong. Never had communion meant more to each of us.

But he was wounded for our transgressions,
he was bruised for our iniquities:
the chastisement of our peace was upon him;
and with his stripes we are healed.

—ISAIAH 53:5

It's your blood that cleanses me, it's your blood that
gives me life.

—WORDS AND MUSIC BY MICHAEL CHRIST. © 1985
MERCY/VINEYARD PUBLISHING

27

PRISON MINISTRY IN BANGKOK

MARGARET COLE

ON OUR ANNUAL return to Southeast Asia, we would fly to Bangkok, stay for a few days of jet lag, and meet new and old friends at the Alliance Guest Home. For many years, our path would cross with an older woman from Southern California who lived at the guesthouse several months each year and eagerly welcomed us.

Margaret Cole was legendary to us and many others. She was in her upper seventies and totally about her Father's business.[1] She was tall and solidly built, but what made her really stand out in Thailand was her red wig. Also, after suffering from some hip trouble, Margaret added a cane to her snappy outfits; when she crossed major intersections, she reminded us of Moses crossing the Red Sea! She turned heads wherever she went.

Sharon and I often met Margaret at the dining room table, where she was eager to share her latest stories. Her conversations always

---

1 Margaret Rice Cole's book "Never Too Old for God" is still available online. She wrote a second book of her adventures in following God after she was sixty and used the proceeds to help finance her projects in several countries. Not only did she feed orphans in Sri Lanka and help start a school for the blind in Thailand, but she also smuggled Bibles into three countries.

centered on Jesus and what He was up to. Sometimes her exuberant chatter made other guests uncomfortable, so the hostess started seating us by Margaret on a regular basis. We loved her tales and wished our zeal for the Lord was more like hers.

One bright morning, she told us about her plans for the day. She was off to a prison to minister to illegals who had been arrested, most of them for overstaying their visas or for drug possession. Did I want to go with her? All the unknowns of the situation made me a little nervous, but I agreed to go.

Our first task was to buy fresh fruit and gather up any Bibles we could find. Then we made our way a long two blocks to the bus stop. Even at 9:00 a.m., Bangkok is hot, so the oranges and Bibles felt heavy. I suggested we take a taxi to the correctional center; my experience taught me you could get across the whole city in a taxi for a few dollars. There might be a little air conditioning for the ride that way. Margaret's response was if I had that much money, we should buy more fruit for the prisoners! On we walked to the bus stop with our arms aching and feet burning as we joined the gathering crowd.

As we boarded the bus, the first thing I noticed was there were no seats. We all stood, crowded, hanging onto straps that hung from the bus roof. I thought the trip would never end, bumping into other people, trying not to fall or lose my precious cargo.

When Margaret announced that we had reached our destination, I was greatly relieved. Once off the bus, we began to fight traffic to cross the street. Four very long blocks later, we saw the sign for the correctional center. A man with a rifle in hand stood on guard at the entrance. We approached him as he announced that visiting hours were closed for lunch, so we would need to wait for an hour. Margaret acted like she didn't hear him, went right past the guard to the closed gate, and called to the guard inside as I hurried to keep up with her. "Little old lady needs to use the bathroom, please," she pleaded. The guard conceded and told us when we were through to come right back to that area. She thanked the man and we went inside to the restroom. After a few minutes, Margaret peeked out the door. All the guards were off on their lunch break. "Come on," she said, "let's go!" She led me the opposite way of the front gate and headed toward a very large sign that said in Thai and English, "No unauthorized personnel beyond this sign." Margaret ignored the sign and kept right on going.

She led me up a large concrete staircase. Many women saw her coming and rushed to the screened area to be near where we were. Margaret greeted them even as she kept walking. "I'm sorry, I can't spend time with you today," she told them. "I taught you about Jesus last year; this year, I have to teach your husbands. It's their turn."

On we went up another long flight of stairs, where once again we were met with a large crowd who were eager to see my friend. The men were from many countries; it was obvious that she cared for them, and they loved her back.

Out of nowhere, a stool appeared. Margaret set up her teaching materials, fruit, and storybooks and began to teach as the many men stood quietly behind the wire barrier. Margaret held court from her little perch, telling them the story of Jesus's love for them.

The lunch hour was now over, so a guard came up the stairs. Shock came over his face as he said, "How did you get up here?"

"Oh," Margaret replied innocently, "the guard at the gate let us in."

After she finished her teaching, Margaret completed her ministry by distributing stamps, writing materials, letters from their loved ones, and even medicines. She was the lifeline for these men. I saw how and why these prisoners met Jesus; His servant was about her Master's business.

We walked out of that prison as though we were part of the employees. Margaret told me there was yet another floor she needed to visit on next year's Thailand trip. A day with her was an experience to remember!

> The righteous shall flourish like the palm tree: he
> shall grow like a cedar in Lebanon.
> Those that be planted in the house of the Lord shall
> flourish in the courts of our God.
> They shall still bring forth fruit in old age; they shall
> be fat and flourishing;
> To shew that the Lord is upright: he is my rock, and
> there is no unrighteousness in him.

> —Psalm 92:12–15

Part 3
Israel

28

JERUSALEM, JERUSALEM

BIKES FOR BOYS

IT WAS OUR second trip to our beloved Israel. My first visit was on my first trip around the world. I knew no one in the Middle East, but when I left Africa on my way there, a seasoned missionary asked where I'd be staying in Jerusalem. "I have no clue," was my reply.

"Oh, my," she said, "you must go to Christ Church Guesthouse. It's right inside the Jaffa Gate in the Old City of Jerusalem. That's where Christians gather, and it would be a good place to contact missionaries." It was advice I'm glad I took. Christ Church was in a great location, and I met wonderful people there from many countries.

The second trip was in 1980. A pastor from Victoria encouraged Sharon and me to connect with missionaries their church had sent out. That couple opened many other doors of ministry for us and taught us much about walking by faith. They lived with their three sons in an apartment in the Old City of Jerusalem, very near Hezekiah's Tunnel (2 Kings 20:20). Those narrow streets—more like passageways—were confusing; it was easy to get lost. This couple showed us it was possible with the love of Jesus to have friends who were Arab, Palestinian, and Jewish. We met many passionate people who thought you had to choose just one group to love and work with; they modeled otherwise.

Our host culture, the Jewish people, often seemed to us to be impatient and in a hurry. However, we had no idea of the pressures of their everyday life. Rumors of war were a part of their daily news. As one missionary told us, if she could make it through the week without losing her temper even in the grocery store, she counted it a good week. Coming from Canada, where people were known for their quiet politeness, we weren't sure how to respond to these people God loves and chose for His own. The local Arabs seemed friendlier, but we couldn't tell how much of their attention was based on wanting some of our money. Still, we reminded ourselves, we were there on assignment; our goal was to see what God was doing in Israel and how His children were bringing His kingdom to earth in that part of the world. And we were called to love those we met.

Behind the stone walls and into the home of our new Canadian friends, the atmosphere became totally different. Marge felt called to a forty-day fast as she wrote a book. Jim was out among the people. Their three sons were adjusting well and seemed to have some good friends among the neighbor children.

One day, Sharon and I were out exploring the area as Jim was returning from his afternoon meetings. The three boys were outside at play when they saw their dad coming through the narrow stone passageway. Immediately, they ran to him with one purpose.

"Abba, Abba," they said, calling him by the Hebrew term of endearment that means "Daddy." "We want bikes! We need bikes!" From their perspective, it seemed like all the kids had bikes except the three boys from Canada. We stood as silent witnesses, frozen there, watching the scene play out. We had been around the family long enough to know there was no extra money for bicycles. Jim and Marge filled our hearts with stories of God's faithfulness, especially in daily provisions. We wondered how they were supported, but they never talked about it. The Lord began to show us, though, as our frequent cash gifts were used to put bread on their table and gas in their van. We had firsthand experience watching our Father provide daily for His children. How was this loving *abba* going to tell his sons that there was no money for any extras?

Jim listened to their urgent pleas and said, "I think that's a great idea, guys. Why don't we pray right here and ask our Father if we can have some bikes?" We watched as the four of them sat down on the flagstone entryway, held hands, and talked to the God of the universe. The prayer was natural—no pleading or explaining, just a simple request for the bikes. Soon, the kids were back at play, and Jim took us into the apartment to join Marge. We were so touched to see Jim teach his kids to trust in their heavenly Father when their earthly dad was not able to come through for them financially. We wondered how to help but heard no direction to enter into the problem. We did not know the Holy Spirit was already at work and did not need our participation.

Sometime after we returned home to Canada, we had a note from Marge telling us the next chapter in the story of the bikes. Three new bikes arrived by mail a month later. Apparently, God had spoken clearly to a woman in Toronto. "The Jones boys in Jerusalem need bikes. Send them." She quickly obeyed the directions she received.

What a God we serve! The bikes had been mailed *before* the request was made. I was reminded of the verse "…Your heavenly Father knoweth you have need of all these things" (Matt. 6:32b). Praise you, Lord Jesus!

29

TOURISTS IN ISRAEL

JOKE AND LORRIE

WE WERE ON yet another trip to Israel, joined this time by our friends Joke and Lorrie. It was sometime in the mid-1980s. This was their first trip to Israel; I strongly encouraged them to go, because I've never felt the same toward the scriptures or my relationship with the Lord since I experienced the land of the Bible and the places Jesus walked. It also helped me to pray more for the peace of Jerusalem.

As Christian leaders, I wanted Lorrie and Joke to feel the same way. We were all looking forward to this time together.

Our flight to Tel Aviv was on El Al Airlines. This was years before all the security delays with x-ray machines and shoe removal that is now normal in America, so when that was instituted in the United States, we knew where they sent the airport workers for training: El Al, Israel's national airlines. The near-constant terrorist threats forced the tiny country to excel in detecting potential problem passengers; it was truly a life-or-death situation for them.

The four of us were getting ready to board our flight in New York when they separated us and started their rough interrogations. Their assumption was guilty until proven innocent. We were excited to go to their country and, as Christians, tried to represent our God well by being gracious and patient. The Israelis, though, were all business and so demanding Joke was in tears.

"Don't you want people to visit your country?" I asked.

"Do you want to get there alive? We have to be sure you aren't a terrorist," was the curt reply. So we dutifully answered their multiple questions and were finally let aboard.

Since this was our third trip to Israel, Sharon and I thought we knew our way around the small country well enough to rent an economy car and be our own guides. Israel is roughly the size of New Jersey or Oregon's Willamette Valley, so you can visit many biblical sites in a single day. With our own little car, it didn't take us long to realize everyone in Israel seemed to be in a hurry. Car horns blared constantly; if we were in the front of the line at a stoplight, and the red light turned yellow (yes, they do that in Israel), and we were not already inching toward the intersection, there were multiple angry honks behind us. Parking was impossible. As one missionary explained, people park on the sidewalks and walk on the streets. Our hotel granted us a parking space, but much of the time it was taken when we got there. All the frenzy after quiet Sweet Home with its four traffic lights helped us decide it would be great to leave Jerusalem for a day.

We headed east toward Jericho. The desert was littered with burned-out tanks--now rusted--remnants of recent wars. I had hoped we could follow the Jordan River north, but instead the road went through towns away from the river. On we traveled. There were Mount Gerizim and Mount Ebal in Samaria; we recalled the blessings and curses God spoke of there to his people (Deut. 27–28).

After several hours of travel, we were ready for a coffee break. A town appeared east of the road, and we eagerly headed toward it; it was called Jenin. We'd never heard of it, but as we entered, it seemed like a normal Israeli village. All we were looking for was a good cup of coffee and maybe a pastry alongside. We finally saw a shop that looked like a restaurant, so we jumped out of our little rental car and headed in.

That time of the year, it was chilly in Israel. We dressed practically and normally for cold weather at home—colorful sweatshirts and matching sweatpants. But we were not in North America! Looking back now and picturing four fair-skinned women dressed in rainbow-colored sweats from head to toe, I can't imagine how we must have looked to the locals.

I think Sharon reached the proprietor first. He was standing behind a display of delicious-looking pastries that whetted our appetites. She greeted him and asked if we could have a table for four. He stood there and didn't speak for a moment.

"No," he finally said, "I can't give you a place to sit."

That's odd, we thought—why not? We turned around to follow the nod of his head. "Only men are drinking coffee here." Sure enough, as we looked into the smoky room through the doorway, we saw that it was filled with men. We began to see the picture a little more clearly.

"Do you know where you are?" he asked pointedly but not unkindly.

"Of course," we answered. "Jenin." We had a map, we weren't lost—we knew exactly where we were.

"Yes." He nodded as he looked closely at us. "Where are you from?" he asked politely.

We told him we were from America and Canada. He might have guessed by our colorful attire.

"Ah," he said, leaving out volumes, we were to learn later. His Arab hospitality kicked in, and he offered to bring us coffee right there in the bakery and to give us free pastries as well. We tried to refuse, but his kindness won us over. Soon, we were drinking coffee and eating our treats, standing near his front door. How naïve we were, four very white Western women standing in front of the clear glass window so any passersby could see us. Later, we drove off raving about how nice the man was to serve us Turkish coffee and insist on giving us the pastries at no cost. We loved the hospitality of the Arab culture.

On we traveled to the Mount of Transfiguration and looked across the future battlefield where Jesus comes to rescue Israel. Matthew 24 was much on our minds as we headed toward Nazareth.

That evening, back in Jerusalem, we joined American friends for dinner. Twenty years earlier, the couple had met Jesus and traveled to Israel to live and work at a kibbutz (an Israeli commune). They were young and adventurous and loved Israel. Now, decades later, they had married and raised their children in this little war-torn country. Arieh and Hannah Amit were true Christian pioneers in the land.

Excitedly, we told them about our day trip and especially the highlight, our time in Jenin. There was dead silence as we related our unusual experience. Finally, Arieh asked us, "Didn't you realize that this city is dedicated to the destruction of the Jewish state? It's a stronghold for Arab terrorists!" He checked the day's newspaper headlines. "There's not a story here today, but often there is news about terrorist acts coming out of Jenin."

All four of us were speechless. Now we could see the dilemma we placed our Arab friend in as he carefully tried to shield us from harm. Now we could see how God protected His bumbling servants who could have made excellent hostages. Now with eyes wide open, we saw the wonderful hand of our Father's care for the four of us.

Thank you, Jesus, for your continual care. You alone can turn the heart, and we are grateful.

Pray for the peace of Jerusalem:
"May those who love you be secure.
May there be peace within your walls
and security within your citadels."

—Psalm 122:6,7 (NIV)

30

Fourth Trip to Israel

After we returned from our trip to Israel with Lorrie and Joke, many of our friends told us they would like to see their spiritual home as well. We worked long and hard with a travel company, and finally the day arrived: off we would fly to Israel with some good friends from Canada and the US for the trip of a lifetime. It would include a celebration of the biblical Feast of Tabernacles, a gathering of people from around the globe, and continue with Arieh (pronounced like the letters R, E, A) giving us a personal look at his adopted country.

We were so pleased that a representative from the travel agency was going to accompany us—that is, until we got to the airport and were informed that the travel agency was now bankrupt, and our trip was canceled.

"No," we said, "you have our money. We are taking the trip."

"No," they said, "there is no money."

"Yes," we said, "we are getting on the plane."

After many phone calls to headquarters, the young woman who was to accompany us finally agreed we could fly to Israel, but we could only stay three days. That was the beginning of a daily struggle with the organization. By a miracle, our trip lasted the full twelve days; it was a wonderful experience for our friends, and Sharon and I learned a lot about perseverance!

Part of the time we spent in Israel was with Arieh and Hannah Amit as our hosts. They showed us glimpses of Israel that most tourists miss. One highlight was staying in a date grove at harvest time. We were on the eastern shore of the Sea of Galilee, far from crowded city streets and surrounded by rural beauty. Huge date palms lined wide walking paths along the water's edge. We loved being there.

We hardly had our bags unpacked when a big machine entered our grove and began shaking those great date palms. All of a sudden, sticky dates were falling everywhere, and the grounds were literally covered with the gooey fruit. In minutes, the tree shaker was done, so pickers spread throughout the grove. They brought in large boxes that were about four feet square. In no time, the pickers gathered the harvest, filled the boxes, and carted them away. Once again, our home for the night turned into a peaceful campground. To our blessing, many dates were left behind for us to share. Tree-ripened fruit; does it get any better?

The following morning, I awoke early and decided to take a morning walk along the shore of the Galilee. There, Jesus had walked. It felt like He was there just as He had been over two thousand years ago. The memory of the colors of the seashore as the water lapped lazily on the beach still makes my heart sing. It is such a privilege to walk where Jesus walked. Friends, don't miss this opportunity if God calls you to visit Israel.

Jesus's early life was centered in Nazareth, and this was a spot we had to see. Here, a bustling city gave little signs of a mighty Savior who had come to earth two thousand years ago to save His people, though today there are many Christians living there. The large city church in Nazareth was much like cathedrals throughout the world;

buildings once brimming with life, in many cases now, are little more than museums. Soon, we were on our way back to our orthodox Jewish hotel in Jerusalem.

> This is what the LORD Almighty,
> the God of Israel, says:
> "When I bring them back from captivity,
> the people in the land of Judah
> and in its towns will once again use these words:
> 'The LORD bless you, you prosperous
> city, you sacred mountain.'"

—JEREMIAH 31:23 (NIV)

Part 4
Back To The United States

31

A Home for His Daughters

Move from Canada

I t was time to renew our visas to live in Canada. Victoria was our beloved home from 1979 to 1988, even though we spent weeks and even months on the road or overseas. We were definitely Americans, but we loved the place where God moved us.

I was invited to teach at an interdenominational Bible school that opened there in the spring of 1979. Sharon joined me that June, and through the following years, we also helped out in two local churches. We began with temporary visas that we had no trouble renewing yearly, as we were not on salary. We weren't taking paying jobs away from any Canadians, so there were no problems until year ten.

As the time approached to renew the documents, we went to the Ministry of Immigration. We had not prayed much about this, as our lives were busy and full. Visa renewal had never been a problem before, so it did not occur to us that God might have other plans.

The officer we met with was the husband of one of our faithful Bible-school students. He greeted us warmly, welcoming us into his office. He listened carefully as we told him about our work. After we finished, he rocked back in his chair, thought awhile, and said, "I'm very sorry, but I cannot renew your visas."

We were shocked and speechless.

"Ladies," he said kindly, "you're asking me to renew your temporary visas for a *tenth year*. We all know that ten years is *not* temporary. The only way I can give you a visa would be for you to swim ashore as a refugee, pay a hundred thousand dollars for citizenship, or come in as domestic help. Esther, with a PhD behind your name, the government is not going to believe you want to be a maid!"

Even though I had been born in Alberta, I had been born to American parents. When it came time to vote, I'd lived in America for many years. It didn't occur to me that a day might come when claiming Canadian roots might be of help. Still, that would have left Sharon without a way to join me.

We walked back to the car in silence. What was God doing? Months earlier, I had begun to get what I call "niggles." God began to give me little feelings of coming change. We were living in a brand-new daylight basement apartment in the house of friends, where we enjoyed the beauty of Victoria and our wonderful Canadian Christian family. Earlier that year, Sharon had returned from visiting her family in Nebraska. While she was there, she heard God's gentle voice ask her one question: *Are you willing to move to Sweet Home?*

Oh no, she thought. She had visited my childhood home with me several times, and it always seemed dark and dreary. Still, she knew the answer Father was looking for. When she returned to Canada, she asked if I had heard anything about moving to Oregon. "How did you know?" I replied. And now this—a closed door to our beloved adopted country. Could it be the end of nine great years in Canada?

Dad and Allie had a small, old house in Sweet Home, Oregon— more like a cottage in size—in the Willamette Valley. It was our home when I was in high school, but all of us Bennetts had moved on and away from there. None of the family thought the house was livable anymore. At one time, I begged Dad to sell it as the neighborhood grew less and less desirable. I remembered his answer. "Who knows?" he said. "Maybe someday you will need this house."

My smart retort was, "Over my dead body would I ever live there." Now those words came back to haunt me; never say never.

We did not have anywhere else to go. Slowly, over the years, Sharon and I had moved everything to our apartment in Victoria, and now it looked as if we had no options other than the little house below three mills in that depressed logging town. In our daily Bible readings, though, it seemed like God rewrote the Bible. Suddenly, every page had verses about the poor. God loves the poor. God loves the widows and orphans. On and on the verses came, highlighting His heart to care for the needy. We always visited the mission field before; now we could see part of our ministry would be in America among the needy. Two friends filled their pickup trucks with our belongings, and we drove our cars onto the Coho ferry for the move in January 1988.

After tearful good-byes, our friends returned north. They told us later that their hearts were breaking as they prayed for us on their journeys home. We, on the other hand, had so much to do that our minds and hearts were filled with unending lists. Where to start?

The old place needed a complete makeover. Dad bought the house in the 1940s from a man who had pieced it together with scraps he brought home from the mill. Where he lived meant little to my father—he was all about building God's kingdom, not houses on earth. If he had a fairly comfortable chair, a good woodstove, and a table nearby for reading material, he was content. My stepmother adjusted to his quirks, so they lived for decades in the small house with no upgrades. That was not my style, though; everything in me was about improving wherever I lived. My mind was always adjusting, changing, remodeling. I had almost met my match with this project.

Demolition was in order. Old metal and glass cabinets needed to come out of the kitchen. Dear Garry, our former landlord in Victoria, started heaving almost everything out onto the rain-soaked grass.

The young man who lived across the street watched as we worked one full day trying to remove all the old kitchen flooring. When

Allen saw our slow progress, he and a buddy came in and tore out the remainder in two hours. It astounded us what two guys on some kind of drug could accomplish in two hours! It was probably speed; it sure looked like it.

As folks began to help us make the place livable, I wandered outside to see the garden area. A five-year-old shouted to me from across a huge mud hole in the street. "Hey, lady," the barefoot boy yelled, sitting on his bike. "Got a cigarette?" I asked him why he wanted one. "My mom needs it. She's out," was the answer.

I invited him in out of the rain and found out his name was Brandon. He told me he lived around the corner. I looked at his muddy jeans and thin T-shirt; he wasn't even aware that his body was shaking in the cold. We had just met our first needy child, and our hearts melted. Sharon was ready to start a laundry service, but instead we filled him with cookies, told him we couldn't help with the cigarette shortage, and sent him on his way. Picking up rocks on the former riverbed that was our side yard became Brandon's part-time job; fifty cents a wheelbarrow suited him just fine and gave us a lot of time to pour love into him.

Meanwhile, friends from Washington and Canada started to make the long trek down I-5 to our little logging town. Each brought skills, love, labor, and help to our new residence. None of them thought of themselves as missionaries, but even though they didn't cross an ocean, they had definitely entered the mission field.

With all the kitchen cabinets recycled to the outside storage room, replacing them was a priority. One day, we headed to Albany to see what we could find. Just leaving town was a great relief for us, so we enjoyed this kind of field trip. A family-owned building supply store (this was long before Home Depot arrived) called Pay-n-Pak was our first stop. They had lots of beautiful cabinets, but the prices stopped us in our tracks: just one cabinet was about two hundred dollars. We were not prepared to put out that kind of money to line our kitchen with cabinets.

As we were about to leave, Sharon noticed several large boxes at a checkout stand, with a clerk just shaking his head at them. "What's that?" she asked him.

"You'll never believe it," the clerk said. It seemed a customer had purchased a full set of kitchen cabinets ten years earlier and had never taken them out of the boxes. "And he still had the *receipt!*" the man said in total disbelief. We looked at each other and looked back at the clerk.

"Would you want to sell them?" we asked.

The man waved his arm across the boxes. "You want 'em? You can take them all for two hundred, as is." We were looking at ten cabinets, upper and lower—a whole kitchen full, exactly the sizes we needed. Our God had someone store the cabinets for us for ten years, awaiting our arrival. They needed assembly, but so did everything else in our world those days. That's how God began to rebuild our home and rebuild some lives along the way.

> Every good and perfect gift is from above, coming
> down from the Father of the heavenly lights, who
> does not change like shifting shadows.
>
> —JAMES 1:17 (NIV)

32

HOPE CENTER

D AD'S OLD HOUSE was built in 1935 and was worse than we could have imagined. There was no city water and the well was dry, so a new well needed to be drilled immediately. God sent one of His young sons to help with that crisis, and thus we made our first new friend. Taking on that project as if it were his own home, Mike quickly discovered we had more than water issues: The electrical system was a firetrap and needed immediate repair. A whole-house renovation began. Everything was a colossal challenge. New church friends tried to help, while neighborhood druggies tore out the old stuff. We thought we were there to help people, but at this stage, we needed all kinds of people to help *us*.

When we moved back to the States in January 1988, we learned that Sweet Home had two seasons: wet and dry. Sharon and I arrived right in the middle of the wet season. I don't think it stopped raining once that year from January until May. Our pathetic home looked just like most of the others in our neighborhood—soggy with junk everywhere and no storage space.

Friends came from as far away as Canada to help update the 1940s-style kitchen. I remember Don sitting on the floor, trying to figure out how to level those countertops. He asked us if we wanted them level with the ceiling or the window ledge or the floor, since all were different. He was pretty challenged. I had visited his home in Victoria; it was a picture-perfect log house he built himself. Still, he kept a good attitude and labored on for a whole week, doing an outstanding job and making our kitchen look as good as it could. A little while later, a carload of lady friends also came down from Victoria to help make this house a home for us. They were a great encouragement too.

Slowly, kids started to come for cookies, woodstove warmth, and Bible stories. Sometimes, we would wash jeans and T-shirts and muddy socks as we gave out hugs to smelly little people. These were our neighbors—children without much guidance who were exposed to drugs, divorce, incest, and hopelessness. This was a new world for us, far from our lives as single women in the beautiful city of Victoria.

We began to call, write, and beg for prayer, wisdom, and lots of love from beyond the city borders. What to do? God continued to bring helpers. Those who came repaired our house and went with us to Gleaners, where we volunteered to receive food to distribute to needy people. Sometimes, that meant gleaning in the fields; always it meant going into some dicey living situations. Drugs so clouded people's minds that they often wouldn't get off the couch to receive the food that came to them; blurry eyes stayed glued to TV sets when we came to the door. One visitor who accompanied Sharon on her Gleaner rounds took several days to recover from the raw sights and sounds of life in our neighborhood. Children ran wild, expecting little from their parents. What they seemed to be raised on was terrible language, little love or training, and certainly no Christian influence.

Our first summer there, several young adults from Victoria volunteered to lead a daily vacation Bible school for us. We held it in our backyard and invited all the kids in our area. One good thing about Gleaners and our backdoor cookie ministry was that it opened the door to all those homes. The parents of those children didn't mind us taking them off their hands for a few hours. Nobody in our area could afford babysitters or daycare, so the backyard VBS served as a blessed relief.

A nearby street was so full of druggies and questionable men that we were fearful to deliver our Gleaners' food boxes alone. We prayed daily for years that the city would make improvements on that unpaved, dead-end road and heal the dead-end lives of those who lived there in the shadows. The day finally came when God made it clear to Sharon that she was never to make the Gleaner rounds again by herself. Shortly thereafter, my brother Jim took over the route and kept it for years, praying his way into the hearts and homes of those needy people. Several years after Sharon stopped the deliveries, a man was murdered at one of the houses on her route.

As Sharon was reading Psalm 91 one day, she felt the Lord highlighting a certain verse. It said, "You will tread on the lion and the cobra; you will trample the great lion and the serpent" (Ps. 91:13 NIV). We knew a key drug dealer lived next door and another across the street. Our phone calls to the police when we were watching drug deals out our kitchen window accomplished nothing. Now God was saying we would tread on and trample our spiritual enemies? We tucked that promise away in our hearts and waited.

Not long after that, we heard of a strange incident. A neighbor from one street over had a wreck on his motorcycle near Sweet Home and died. He was the father of four small children who came to a Bible class at our house, so the teenager who taught it went with Sharon to his graveside service. As the casket was about to be lowered into the ground, the man's friends placed his jacket on top. Sharon's heart stopped. She had no idea this man was a member of the Hell's

Angels motorcycle gang. There, on the back of his jacket, was the insignia: a cobra. We had prayed many times for that family, with no idea the dad's life would come to such an abrupt end. The wife and children soon moved away to start a new life.

We went for walks uptown just to be able to leave the depressing area where we lived. Our street had no sidewalks or pavement and only one streetlight for a five-block area, so we tried to go to more pleasant surroundings. Near the downtown area, there was an old Baptist church for sale. I told Sharon stories of years earlier when my dad helped build that church structure. We often prayed for its protection, as it had been on the market for a long time. "Father," we would pray, "please use this building for Your kingdom." Then we would continue on our walk.

One day, a surprising answer came. *You buy it*, we thought He said. I can't begin to list all the reason two ladies with no salary or guaranteed income did *not* need an old, rundown church. Just getting into the building and walking through the four floors with ten thousand square feet was overwhelming. There was also the badly dated, three-bedroom parsonage next door, with the five small city lots that came with the church. Had we known the real condition of the buildings, I am sure we would never have obeyed that green bean Voice.

Our dear friends, the Kyles, volunteered their home as a meeting place to bring a few folks together to discuss this possible project. We began to meet every Friday night to pray and try to discern why God would want us to buy this church property. Everyone knew Sweet Home had a gigantic problem with battered and abused women who seemed to always have two or three little ones clinging to them. The nearest women's shelter was in Corvallis, about a forty-five-minute drive away. Women who were fleeing abusive relationships seldom had decent transportation to make that kind of trip. Plans began to form for a women's shelter.

With that prayer backing, Sharon and I went to the pastor of the church that was for sale. His congregation now met in a good-looking building farther out of town. He gladly showed us around their old building and told us the price: $150,000. We were pretty sure we could buy most of Sweet Home for that amount of money! Congress had just passed the Spotted Owl legislation; it effectively put a Closed for Business sign on all the local forestlands. It was a hard time to be a logger and a tough time to ask for financial help in a logging town. With the woods almost entirely closed down, people were depressed, and poverty worsened. We thanked the pastor for his time and went back to the weekly prayer meetings.

Months passed, and we made our second appointment to see the pastor. We told him all about the need we saw that his buildings could fill. We reminded him of the insurance he was still paying for the place and pointed to the stained-glass window that was vandalized. The pastor was getting nervous, and no offers had come in. Our Friday-night prayer group worked hard behind the scenes, which must have had some influence, as the price was now down to $100,000. We left still knowing we had no funds, as we were still trying to get our own little house into decent living order.

More time, more prayer. One of the things Sharon and I insisted upon was that we would be tithing to other ministries on whatever financial gifts came in for this new project. Many of our prayer group disagreed. Why would we give away money when we didn't have enough for our needs? Weren't the people donating to HOPE? Why would we pass their gifts on to others? We tried to explain God's principle of finances: give and you shall receive, that your joy may be full. The discussions continued that night and resulted in some of our friends choosing to leave the project. Those who stayed never questioned God's principles again as we watched Him refill our coffers time and time again after every tithe and gift went through our hands to other ministries.

We made another appointment to see the pastor. We felt like Moses going back to Pharaoh as once again we presented the need and desperate state of the lost women and hopeless children. Grudgingly, he dropped the price to $75,000. It might as well have been $750,000. More prayer. More waiting.

It was time for a return visit with Pastor Chuck. "Are you willing to stand before God and tell him you told us no?" I boldly asked.

He could not contain his anger any longer. "I promised my people if they would help us pay for our new building, they would be paid back when we sold the old one," he blurted out.

"How much did you borrow from your congregation?"

"$42,100."

"We will give you $42,100 for that building then, but here are the conditions. We will pay no interest and will give you the money in full in one year."

I think he was so glad to be rid of us that he agreed. There was only one stipulation: We were not to use the building for Sunday-morning church services. We had no intention of planting a church there, so we agreed and left in awe. What had I just said? What did we just sign up for? How were we, two missionary women, going to come up with $43,000?

At the next Friday-night prayer meeting, we began to strategize, and thus began God's miracles of blessing and provision. We would all get to know God a lot better in the coming year. Desperation with deadlines can be a good teacher.

Next on the agenda was a shout-out for help far and wide. Can you come help? We knew we needed to approach local churches besides our friends from afar. We made an appointment to visit a nearby pastor. He greeted us cordially and then carefully moved behind his desk, putting a natural barrier between us even as he tried to be understanding. He finally said, "We'll pray for you, and maybe some of our men will volunteer to help you, but I'm sorry, we can't provide any money right now." Many of the people of that church were a wonderful blessing. For years, they gave sacrificially of their time, energy, and money.

The impossible project had begun.

> But my God shall supply all your need according to
> his riches in glory by Christ Jesus.

> —PHILIPPIANS 4:19

33

ALLEN'S STORY

HELP FROM THE NEIGHBORHOOD

> O LORD, thou hast brought up my soul from the
> grave; thou hast kept me alive, that I should not go
> down to the pit. Sing unto the LORD, O ye saints
> of his, and give thanks at the remembrance of his
> holiness.
>
> PSALM 30:3–4

WE SURVEYED OUR new treasure. The slim bank account we opened in faith for HOPE Inc. (Helping Our People in Emergency) reflected the needy town, as challenges met us on every front. The once attractive front entrance to the church was cracked and crumbling. The sanctuary wasn't too bad, considering it was over forty-five years old and built by volunteers, but we didn't dare let anyone sit in the balcony, the fire department told us. The plumbing was in miserable condition, and since the electricity was installed in the 1940s, there were whole rooms with no electrical outlets. The former parsonage next door was last used for youth groups who had painted some of the walls black. Floor coverings, landscaping—everywhere we looked we saw long to-do lists. The walls were deteriorating badly in several places, and the roof had to be replaced. And what a steep pitch there was to that roof! Never mind we were talking about housing the homeless; this place had to be up to code before anyone could spend the night.

The crew for the roof demolition primarily came from the other side of the tracks—our neighborhood. Those unshaven, grubby-looking men were desperate for employment, so they came and worked hard for minimum wages. I have never seen such demolition. They tore that old roof off so fast, roofing material flew everywhere. Other volunteers gladly picked up the debris and watched those guys get more done in a few hours than our careful workers would have accomplished in days. They were grateful for the free lunches too.

Allen was our lead demolition expert. He and his wife (barely twenty-one) lived across the street from us with their family that consisted of three preschoolers, a toddler and a baby. Their lives were an ongoing nightmare. We started reaching out to them when we first arrived; the kids were open to handouts, and the couple knew they could borrow our phone. Their wars were so loud that we could not help but hear and pray.

Since we were not savvy about drug abuse, we didn't realize Allen's life was accelerating out of control. One day, he left and began a crazy downward spiral. For two weeks, he lived on drugs—no food at all. His wife was beside herself with worry. While she was paralyzed with depression, their kids ran wild. We prayed daily about how to proceed. Should we give her bus money to take the kids and flee back to her mom in another state?

One day toward evening, I noticed a young man walking down the street toward their house. That wasn't unusual—they often had drop-ins—although this man didn't look like their normal friends.

The young man went into the house, but we never saw him leave. With no sidewalks and the old houses built close to the road, our houses were just feet apart. Oh no, we thought; has she found a new boyfriend already? Our hearts sank. What a mess!

The next morning, we went across the street to check on the mom and take the kids a little food. As we stood on the porch talking with her, the mysterious man we had seen the night before walked out to join us.

"Hello, Esther," he said pleasantly.

I turned to look at this man I thought was a stranger. "Do I know you?" I asked.

"I'm Allen," he said, smiling.

Allen? The last time I saw Allen, he was walking down the street in a long black trench coat with his head down, full of long, oily, dark curls, as he pulled on a cigarette. This man in front of me had clear, clean, blue eyes and short, light-brown hair. How could this be?

"I met Jesus in jail," he said, again flashing a giant, boyish grin. I just stood there staring, as did his wary wife. She had been through so much with this man; was this just a new phase? Allen then asked if he could come to our Bible study that evening. Of course, Sharon and I said, filled with wonder at this changed man standing before us. That began an amazing time of transformation. We slowly learned more about what brought him to that point.

Allen's story, unlike many, was that he came from a two-parent family. The challenge, though, was that his dad was a long-haul truck driver. Every time his dad saw a new town that looked interesting, he would move his family there. By seventh grade, Allen had attended over thirty schools and was too dyslexic to spell "cat." Each time he changed schools, he would start over by beating up the biggest guy in his class. That did not make him a friend of his new teachers. He was put on the drug Ritalin at a young age, which he said prepared him for illegal drugs in his teens. He married very young, looking for someone to love, and followed his family's patterns.

That morning as we stood on his doorstep, Allen went on to tell us he experienced hell in the Linn County Jail. When the police picked him up with charges of drug possession, he hadn't eaten for two weeks. His body just went from one high to another on the drugs. Afraid of what would happen if the officers found the drugs he was carrying to sell, he decided to just swallow them. That set off a horrible reaction in his depleted system, and as he was dying, he found himself falling down a greasy, black pit. He cried out to Jesus to save him, and his soul immediately returned to his body. Three times he slid down that long, slick hole. He tried desperately to stop, his fingers digging into the sides, but nothing could stop his fall. "I heard the cries, I felt the heat, and I screamed for mercy, but each time I fell farther," he told us.

Allen was overwhelmed with horror, as he knew for certain he couldn't get out. In his childhood, someone had taken a young Allen to church, and in second grade, he was baptized. This long-lost sheep called out to Jesus again, and this time, he seemed to shoot straight up the tube and out of the hellhole. Immediately, he hit the floor from the upper bunk of his jail cell. "I prayed like I'd never prayed before," he confessed.

He asked a guard for a Bible, saying he had to have one. They brought him a King James Version, and he began to read intently. The boy who could not read at all could now read and understand an older form of English. Moments later, Allen started preaching to the other men in his cell. The man could now read perfectly, and he couldn't stop filling himself with God's Word. "I wept and wept," he told us. "I felt so clean, so new, so different, so saved."

Was Allen one of the reasons God moved us from comfortable Victoria to the back streets of Sweet Home? The call was starting to make sense.

Living across the street from Allen and his family, we got to see his transformation up close. Up and down the streets of Sweet Home he walked, singing "Hail Jesus, You're My King."[1] He knew every drug user and seller in town, and they each heard his story. He invited them to join him at our Bible study. Our small home group took on a whole new look. Hurting, questioning eyes looked at us out of life-hardened faces. We had no idea who these men were or where they came from. All we knew was Allen always brought new faces and aching hearts.

Hope filled our new believers. Allen took his men to witness in all the Sweet Home taverns and other places we had never been.

Almost immediately, he and his friends started joining the work parties at the HOPE Center. It was a fresh start for them to work with nice local churchmen, as well as those who came from afar. God blessed us, and many of us became lifelong friends with that precious changed brother.

> He lifted me out of the slimy pit,
> out of the mud and mire;
> he set my feet on a rock
> and gave me a firm place to stand.
>
> —Psalm 40:2 (NIV)

---

1 "Victory Chant," by Joseph Vogels. © 1985 Scripture in Song/Maranatha! Music. (ASCAP).

34

HELP FOR HOPE

GOD DOES IT AGAIN

A S ALLEN BECAME one of our most trusted workers on the HOPE
Center roof, we were also reaching out to our many friends from
Sharon's home church in Seattle. Three couples drove down with their
campers to spend a long weekend helping us. We found an immediate problem: There weren't enough power outlets to plug in their rigs.
Thankfully, our helpers were retired Boeing engineers; they worked
around the challenges and committed to returning soon. I believe
Dick and MaryAlice Timm made the trip six weekends until the
sprinkler system was installed. That drive was over 250 miles each
way, but Dick was determined to finish that job.

The plumbing updates were an urgent project. Folks came from
Sweet Home as well as out of state to help. Many brought supplies
and dollars to make HOPE Center livable. We went on to learn our
city leaders had no idea what codes we needed to meet if we planned
to house people in the old church building. They finally decided to
treat it as a motel, which meant a lot of work was needed. All of the
ceilings had to be replaced or painted with a fire-retardant mixture.
With ten thousand square feet to cover, that was a huge endeavor.
Dale and Pam Miner spent many, many hours on gigantic ladders

painting over their heads. The special paint cost twenty-five dollars a gallon; they did give us a discount, but the thirsty tiles required a lot of paint. Sheila Kent and others spent hours cleaning reclaimed glass bricks to sell.

Smoke alarms added $5,000 to the $10,000 electricity update and the $10,000 plumbing bill. Offerings came in, and the money flowed out. The fire escape had to be replaced and walkways repaired. The sanctuary needed help. Chester Royer and a crew from Evangelical Church treated HOPE Center like a part-time job, donating countless hours. A building trades class from Sweet Home High School walked over to help every school day for weeks. People painted that old church, caulked the windows, repaired the lawns, replaced old shrubs, added a whole new bathroom, and remodeled the old ones. At last, the old building was taking shape. There was still much to do, but we were on our way. And the fellowship was wonderful. Jeani West and others filled hungry bellies of the workers.

The team wondered how God would help us get the old classrooms converted into living quarters. One nice local pastor asked how his church could help. We sent messages to several other churches in the area and asked them to consider adopting a room to turn it into a warm, welcoming place for a woman in need. We added the incentive of a sign by the room doors honoring the congregations who helped us. The Lutheran, Episcopal, and Catholic churches dove right in. The Catholics even took on two kitchens! Hundreds of work hours later, the HOPE Center started to become a home. It was all finished except for carpeting, so Community Chapel offered to not only purchase the carpet but also have it installed. The second floor looked beautiful.

All this took every dime that was sent in for the ministry. The one-year deadline was looming closer, but what could we do? We were busy submitting to the local building codes and couldn't think about the upcoming balloon payment.

Early on, the former occupants of the building offered their nice, new church building for a fundraiser dinner. People rallied from all across the area to show their support and pledge financial help. Several ladies made homemade cinnamon rolls to sell at the annual Sweet Home Sportsman's Holiday Parade, but a dollar a roll didn't go very far toward our bill. The renovation work went on, and all bills were paid on time, but there was never much left over toward the price of the building. Still, the calendar showed the deadline looming closer.

The Sweet Home *New Era* newspaper shared our upcoming crisis. "HOPE Center Needs Fifteen Thousand Dollars," the headline read. "Payment One Month Off" was the subtitle. Dean Kyle, the much-loved local optometrist, was the board chair and spoke positively in the article about the great need and enthusiastic support. But where was the lump sum going to come from?

When Sharon and I first moved to Sweet Home, we began to pray for the city's five key leaders: superintendent of schools, police chief, mayor, newspaper editor, and fire chief. That led to a great friendship with Alex and Debbie Paul from the *New Era*. Alex, ever the inquisitive reporter, tried to figure out how we lived. "Does God just float down money from heaven?" he joked with us one day. Like us, HOPE had a few regular supporters, but every day brought financial surprises as God touched different hearts. Now, it was the day of reckoning.

The board met at our house to discuss the crisis at hand. The Baptists were nervous; most of the HOPE board was nervous too, but I was calm. That morning, I had received clear direction from the Lord. We sat in quiet tension in a close circle near the woodstove as different ones reiterated the problem. Finally, I told them I thought the Lord had shown me a solution. The board members looked at me expectantly as I began to follow what God had said: I offered to empty out my retirement funds to singlehandedly pay the bill in full.

Everyone gasped. "You can't do that!" our treasurer said. She was my tax accountant and knew my finances well.

"Yes, I can," I said calmly, "and I plan to."

Years earlier, in a church missions board meeting, a friend of ours saw the needs from God's perspective. The board went around and around as they tried to figure out how the church could meet the financial needs of their missionaries. Our friend heard a whisper in his ear that in that very room was enough money to more than meet their mission budget. It was *in their own pockets* if they would be open to give. Now it was our turn.

Our treasurer, Shirley, seeing my determination, said, "OK. We will accept your offer, but HOPE Center will pay you back in full as we are able." That seemed to break open the floodgates. Before the evening was over, every board member gave generously out of their own means. The deadline was met, the Baptists got their money, and HOPE Center would be able to open to help our people in emergency.

Our God is no man's debtor. Sometimes I think God likes crises. It gives Him glory to see His kids come through.

We prayed for workers, counselors, secretaries, and full-time employees. There was no salary to draw people, only a faith promise of room and board as God provided. We spread the word in Canada, asking, "Does anyone feel God calling them to minister in Oregon?"

The first ones to answer the call to move were John and Lynn Wiens and their girls. With Lynn's prayer life and John's graphic art and woodworking skills, they were a real boost to our workload. Their involvement with HOPE spanned decades. They were followed in the parsonage by Howard and Janet Bradley and family. The Bradleys were fresh from a year with Youth with a Mission and wanted to continue in a missionary lifestyle. Howard was amazing with his hands, which was great because everything needed to be repaired, rebuilt, or remodeled. Janet's heart broke for the needy. She simply kept the

HOPE Center full as she poured out love, prayers, and acceptance on the many women and children God brought. Thema Black and many other single women served as live-in staff. Many, many quality people served behind the scenes on the board, fundraising, cooking, praying, cleaning, and working at garage sales. And always, always, broken lives were being made whole as God's kingdom expanded. Many women and children saw their lives take a turn for the better because of one night to a year under that roof.

Early on, Sharon received a call from the State of Oregon with an offer of a $20,000 grant for the HOPE Center. "Women in crisis" was a popular topic, so there were state funds to distribute. There was only one qualification for the money: we must not have any religious paraphernalia in the building—certainly no crosses on the walls. Sharon shook her head as she talked with the woman. "Ma'am," she told her, "we are Christians. The only reason we are doing this is because of our faith. There is no way we can abide by those rules." The government worker was very upset that we refused her offer. The money would have been great, but there was no way to reach a compromise. God never failed us. Every year He paid the bills, sent in all the provisions, provided for the many people, and sent many on their way to a new life.

Twenty-five years have come and gone. We were told in 1990 that the average life of a shelter in Oregon was five years, but the HOPE Center continues to be a beacon for women who need a second chance.

> God will make this happen,
> for he who calls you is faithful.
>
> --1 THESS. 5:24 (NLT)

35

THE SONG SPARROW

THE SONG OF a little bird brought us great hope.

Sharon and I worked and lived among the poor in Sweet Home, Oregon, for six years. In 1994, the Lord opened the door for us to move to a new manufactured home in a more middle-class area of town. Ours was one of the first houses in this new development, so we began claiming our area for God, walking the streets in His name and announcing to our new neighbors that we were the resident missionaries. They were cordial to us and probably a little skeptical. Our good friends Dean and Mary Ann Kyle moved next door four months later, so for quite a few years we enjoyed wonderful Christian fellowship and community living as we wore out the path between our houses.

Our overseas trips continued, including leading eleven friends from Canada and the United States to Tanzania. We visited Jean Wahlstrom and Marvin Kanenan and their work at the Maasai Lutheran Girls Secondary School near the base of Mount Kilimanjaro. It was a wonderful time and fulfilled the desire of many of our group to experience Africa. The Maasai girls needed new red sweatshirts to keep them warm at night, so each of us included a large number of sweatshirts in our luggage.

We returned home in what felt like a funk. Nothing was on the schedule; nothing much was moving in our lives. We had long since resigned from our roles at the HOPE Center; I might have been good at rounding up workers and generating funds, but I was definitely not the right person for the day-to-day happenings at the shelter. I was grateful when God provided others more fitting for the ongoing ministry there. Our friend Alex, the editor of the Sweet Home newspaper, asked, "So what's next?"

"Nothing," I told him. Not a thing was on the horizon. Until the next day.

The phone rang; a man who never called us was on the other end. On behalf of a church we worked alongside for about five years, he asked us a question: Would we possibly be available to return to Victoria and help a congregation we loved so much? It was in crisis. Leave dreary, drippy Oregon to return for a brief stay in Victoria helping people near to our hearts? It was hard to pray with open minds; we were already mentally packing!

Going back to the city that was our home from 1979 to 1988 and seeing many new and old friends with a huge change in scenery was literally heaven sent. If we had to endure the inevitable rainy season that keeps the Pacific Northwest green, it could at least be in Canada's City of Gardens. We were on the way with great expectations.

Victoria welcomed us with sunshine, renewed relationships, and high hopes. It didn't take long to see some of the challenges and hear from hurting hearts. We tried to hear God's voice as clearly as we heard the voices of His people; what was *His* desire in this? Every day we prayed, asking God for our marching orders. We loved reminding our Father of the words in Ephesians 2:10 that assured us that our job was to walk in the good works that <u>He</u> prepared beforehand.

We set out spending time with people. We visited each home group and went on coffee, lunch, and dinner dates with folks. We listened and poured out love and prayers. The church was deeply divided; we seemed to be in the middle of great heartache.

A dear couple opened their basement suite to us. They lived near Witty's Lagoon, a favorite beach destination for many in that area. We could walk along the saltwater that led to Puget Sound, see the Olympic Mountains that reminded us America was not far away, and try to collect our thoughts. Here the swans, ducks, and seagulls seemed to thrive. It felt good to feed them as we cried out to Father for wisdom. Creation was our heart lifter, and we absorbed it fully. Our shoulders felt heavy as we hurt for our suffering friends. It seemed there was no earthly solution in sight as we trudged along the water.

Suddenly, the heavy silence was broken. Where was that beautiful music coming from? A bird was singing a stunning, complicated song. We stopped in our tracks and looked around. Neither of us saw any songbird. There was that melody again; where was it coming from? We were caught up in the glorious strain. What was it? We walked over to a small scrub tree and stood quietly. There was the song again. The only bird we could see in the tree was a sparrow. I had never heard a sparrow sing—I had only heard them chirp. "Do sparrows actually sing?" we asked each other. Well, this one did! We continued to listen, and our hearts began to rejoice. Had Father sent a sparrow to sing to us? Joy flooded our souls, and peace came. He who watches over sparrows was in charge. We knew only Jesus could heal His church; all He wanted us to do was trust Him and follow.

The remainder of those four months often found us back at the lagoon, listening for our small winged friend. Most times he was there, in his bush camouflage, singing his heart out. His beautiful song rang out, but never as precious as that morning of heavy grief, when our hearts were so lifted and encouraged. To this day, my heart rejoices as I think again about God's precious love and care for His children.

Some friends later told us that song sparrows do exist. All I know is that God can easily make a sparrow sing a beautiful song because I heard it, and I thank Him so much for that precious memory.

> He brought me up also out of a
> horrible pit, out of the miry clay,
> and set my feet upon a rock, and
> established my goings.
> And he hath put a new song in my mouth,
> even praise unto our God:
> many shall see it, and fear, and
> shall trust in the LORD.

> —PSALM 40:2, 3

36

CRAWFORDSVILLE TO IDAHO

Major change was in the air, and we had no idea. Things that never crossed our minds were about to come to pass.

It was September 2003. Sharon and I had heard from the Lord that we were not to return to the Philippines or Thailand the following January, as we had most years since 1979. It was hard to believe we were not going to revisit Southeast Asia that year; we couldn't help but wonder what was next.

While living in America, we usually hosted home groups to be involved in ministry, and we welcomed a new couple this soggy October. They were a fine, dedicated couple but were very discouraged. They knew they had a call to missions, but their denomination insisted they practice their ministry skills on Americans before crossing the ocean. For them, that meant moving from a large California city to tiny Crawfordsville, Oregon (population 150 at the time), to try to build up a struggling country church. The church was down to a faithful handful. We offered to fill in for them a few times when they had to be gone, so we knew things were tough.

One day, we got word the young couple had abruptly left. Bad quickly turned to worse as the congregation tried to figure out what to do.

Word from headquarters was that if there was a congregation with a similar doctrine within eight miles (there was), and there were fewer than fifty adults (how about ten?), the church should close. We had already been praying for this struggling group, but now our prayers intensified.

Sharon and I were invited to attend a congregational meeting. Thirty-five people came to let their voices be heard. "Do not close our church!" they pleaded. No one had a plan on how to keep it open, but it sure was their desire.

As we'd prayed for Crawfordsville Community Church, a plan began to formulate, so at the proper time, we brought up our proposal. We offered to fill in for three months. That would get us to the end of the year. At that time, we would all reevaluate. Since there were no other offers on the table, Sharon and I were a shoo-in.

Nine folks came that first Sunday. No one mistook us for a normal pastoral team, and since we had little to no experience of leading a church, we made it very clear that we needed help—a lot of help. We were two missionary women, not clergy. People who had always been in the shadows began to fill the pews and volunteer to serve.

We began to teach God's Word, form a worship team and include a Missions Moment every week to introduce stories of our faithful Father on the mission field. By the start of December, Father had eighteen people coming. That doesn't sound like much but church growth folks get excited when there's a one-hundred-percent increase! Church finances were meager, and a poverty spirit tried to fight for control. Several good men stepped up to serve as elders. Prayer time increased. Big problems like the septic field sent us to the county officials to plead for mercy. Friends from far and wide were praying for us, so we kept on working there, and hope began to rise.

Looking around the church and parsonage brought back memories of HOPE Center. It looked like everything needed to be updated. Just to get into the sanctuary required going up a flight of stairs; getting to the basement for Sunday school and potlucks meant taking even more stairs. Most of the people left in the church found that a real challenge.

Sharon was developing a worship team, and the folks loved the music. She challenged the group to prepare Bible studies to share with each other to help them grow spiritually. We had a smoke break in the middle of the Sunday-morning service so people who had to have a cigarette would be able to come. Pews that had been moved to other parts to the building were making their way back into the sanctuary as attendance increased.

Before we came, several ladies were already involved in Samaritan Purse's Christmas shoebox ministry. That ministry increased; several carloads of people even went one rainy Sunday afternoon to help at the area distribution center, where we dropped off over two hundred boxes of blessings for kids. Food was one of our strengths. One week, we invited a nearby group of Teen Challenge men to share their stories and eat our food. It was such a winning combination that they became a regular addition to our country church.

Our salary started at $150 a month each. Over the next four years, it grew as the congregation increased. We were always careful to tithe the church's offerings to ministries outside our church body. After God worked miracles to get our septic-tank situation solved, I told the church board that we needed to give Him a thank-you offering. They looked at me with questions in their eyes. I suggested we help a country church at the other end of the county that was trying to install indoor plumbing for the first time. When I mentioned I thought it should be $1,000, I almost lost them, but they bravely recovered and chose to trust. I wish I could have been there when that little congregation opened the letter with that check in it! And by God's grace, we never missed the money.

CCC was nearing capacity on holidays. It was great to get to speak to a full house, but I celebrated my seventy-fifth birthday and was getting tired of preaching every week. Sharon had ten on her praise team and was ready for a change as well. Early on, we told the congregation that when God sent a young family, we'd move out of the way. The problem was we knew that wasn't likely to happen, but God surprised us all.

One day, we heard about a young pastor and his family looking for a church to serve. He was available and eager to come. One of our elders drove down to interview him and came back excited. His family would even live in the parsonage that had been empty since the Hurricane Katrina family we hosted fled back down south.

Kelly and Heidi Graham came almost immediately, blending in with our ministry and then taking the reins. What now? We looked around and could not see what our next step should be.

About that time, my niece called from Boise, Idaho, just to chat and share prayer requests. When I told her of the change on our horizon, she surprised me. "I don't know if this is God or not, Aunt Esther," she said, "but how about you and Sharon coming over here to provide spiritual care for my residents and staff?" She owned three senior facilities in Boise and was planning to soon open a fourth. I promised to pray about it.

Years earlier, when God was preparing us to move to Sweet Home, both Sharon and I thought He rewrote the Bible: everywhere we turned, we saw verses about ministering to the poor. This time, however, we kept seeing verses about the desert blooming. No one could ever call Sweet Home a desert; suddenly it looked like we were Boise bound.

In March of 2008, we flew to Idaho to have a look around and see what work and life in the Boise area would look like. We marveled at Linda's beautiful senior facilities; they felt more like four-star hotels we'd seen in Asian cities. We found a great house in Meridian that would be central to all her senior communities, so the move was on. One day after my seventy-sixth birthday, on May 24, 2008, the caravan left Sweet Home to deposit us in Idaho. My car was tucked between two trucks driven by our former church elders. Our twenty-year pilgrimage to Oregon had ended, and a new adventure in Idaho had just begun.

Our ministry/work assignment was to travel to two assisted living residences and one memory care, where we would offer a Christian meeting for people who could not attend their own churches. We knew we couldn't compete with their ideas of what church was supposed to be, but we hoped to bring them God's Word with love and encouragement. Sharon's ministry in music quickly won over the residents; they loved those old hymns. I would bring a short message of encouragement, sprinkling in some faith stories. We began in June of 2008, ministering, teaching, befriending, and helping folks from every denomination or no spiritual background. We've led quite a few memorial services and even officiated at a couple of weddings. After a few years, we also started passing an offering plate; our residents have been able to send hundreds of dollars to various outreach projects. For me, it is a dream job. Sharon finds the work pretty repetitive, but she remains faithful.

May of 2016 marked our eighth year. I needed to cut back on the workload; Linda built two more facilities in the Treasure Valley, so we were on the road four days a week. Reluctantly, we said good-bye to the memory care and two assisted living gatherings and still lead two services a week. We average fifteen to thirty in attendance in each building.

God is so faithful, even as I grow older and weaker. Instead of doing so much travel, dear ones come to us now—missionaries and friends we have known in many countries have found their way to Idaho to rest, encourage us, and share what Father is doing around the world.

It's been an exciting life for both of us. We continue to pray for this old world, tossed and torn, but each day we are assured that God is in charge of everything. We are excited about His next step in all of our lives.

Folks, Jesus is coming soon!

But as it is written: "Eye has not seen, nor ear heard,
Nor have entered into the heart of man
The things which God has prepared for those who
love Him."
But God has revealed them to us through His Spirit.
For the Spirit searches all things, yes, the deep things
of God.

—1 Corinthians 2:9–10 (NKJV)

37

THOUSAND PALMS HOUSE SALE

THE MIRACLES CONTINUE, AND I'M STILL LEARNING

As I've grown older, I would have thought the lessons learned in the past would sustain me in these days where I must depend more and more on the Lord. But I see that isn't necessarily true; I still need to continue to trust Him for everything.

I recently found myself incapable of taking care of two older houses I had purchased as investments some twenty years ago. They were poor investments, and I simply wanted out of the struggle of financial failures. One day, in late summer of 2015, I simply asked Father if He'd please take care of this mess for me.

A couple of days later, the burden returned; what was I supposed to do with those houses? I started to fret and again asked the Lord to do it for me. I taught Psalm 37 in the 1980s, showing people how to live without fretting, but I wasn't practicing it very well.

Almost immediately, I heard His familiar voice. He said simply, *Don't worry about it.* At once I felt relieved; He said not to worry. "Thank you, Father; You're so good to me. I praise You, dear Abba."

Weeks passed, and I began to wonder when He would do something about my California house. The time of it being a nice winter escape for us seemed to be past. I knew if it didn't sell, I'd have to rent it; I recalled my problems in the past with renters, thieves, poor laborers, expensive repairmen, and on and on. It seemed best to go to Thousand Palms and try to figure out what to do onsite.

Sharon and I flew down, knowing we had nine days to solve the problem. I asked my dear friends Howard and Janet Bradley to come lend us a hand. Over the years, the Bradleys often helped us with house and garden repairs. We in turn let them use the house as a vacation destination. This time they arrived two days ahead of us, so by the time we showed up, they were madly cleaning, repairing, and getting everything ready for our arrival. What precious friends and gifts from our heavenly Father; I call them my kids.

Our next day was full of preparation for selling the little aging trailer house. We needed to paint the exterior, shampoo the rugs, get some plumbing things updated—the list kept growing. The clock was ticking, so we called a Realtor. We thought she was exceptional and felt she would do her best for us. She left saying she'd be back in two days to take pictures and get ready for an open house in three days. There was a problem with the painter, though; his promise to paint the house in two days had now stretched to four, and it wasn't even close to done.

I began to fret again and found myself praying in the night about it. We couldn't possibly finish the work and make our scheduled flight back to Boise. With all the repairs going on, I couldn't even find a place to go away and pray, and I needed that now more than anything. If I stepped out on the porch, there were even people working there. I felt tears coming. Didn't He say not to worry? But I *was* worrying, and I knew I wasn't walking in faith.

Just then, I heard my phone, so I went to pick it up. My sister Grace was on the line. We chatted, and almost immediately I began to calm down. She seems to have that effect on anyone around her.

I poured out my frustrations, and she began to ask about the little house. As I told her my reasons for wanting to sell, she said, "Esther, I think Don and I should buy your home."

"You're kidding!" I interjected, just as her husband walked into the room where she was.

"I'll call you right back," she told me as she quickly hung up.

Ten minutes later, Don was on the phone asking questions. Now, I knew he was a good businessman, and I was sure he'd say, "We'd better not." But to my amazement, he said, "We'll take it—my wife wants it." He went on to say, "Grace is giving me a big thumbs-up sign that she's very happy."

I could hardly believe it! I must have mumbled something, because Don repeated, "I told you, we will take it." That's when I recalled that still, small Voice that said, *Don't worry about it*. I now had to humble myself and ask forgiveness. I scolded myself; why do I not trust?

Years ago, in college, I was given a book by J. B. Phillips called *Your God Is Too Small*. I had to admit, it was true. Even after all of my experiences with Him being real in my life, my God was still too small. Is *your* God too small?

Father, thank You for your patience, love, and desire to bring us into a deeper relationship of trust in You.

I started this book by saying I wanted to hear His Voice. I close this book with some weather stories and say I want to trust that still, small Voice. Join me as we grow together, eagerly looking, walking, and rejoicing in His presence.

PART 5
WEATHER PRAYERS

38

LITTLE CLOUD

HELEN AND THE VANCOUVER AIRPORT

HEBREWS 11:6 SAYS, "Without faith it is impossible to please God." That verse was in my heart and on my mind as I daily tried to learn how to walk by faith and not by sight. How did I get this faith so I could please Him? I saw His hand at work over and over on my first world trip, but walking by faith was still not a lifestyle for this practical, feet-flat-on-the-ground PE teacher. A new chapter in this walk began on a trip to Canada.

I had been teaching in Auburn, Washington, most of my career. On weekends, I would often be invited to speak at various Christian women's meetings in the northwest. This particular weekend, I was traveling to Vancouver, British Columbia, to minister at an Aglow meeting. Aglow International was a fairly new organization at that time, formed to introduce women to the Holy Spirit in a deeper way. It was a great way to bring women together from all kinds of backgrounds.

The summer was incredibly beautiful, with clear, blue skies. I-5 was nearly empty as I cruised along in my trusty Pontiac, singing and praising the Lord, when a stray thought went through my mind. I looked up at vast blue sky, and there to my right hung a little white cloud, all alone in all that blue. I had the strangest thought: *Could I get that cloud to move?* When the thought refused to go away, I asked Father to move that baby cloud to the other side of my car. Nothing happened, but I felt urged to pursue the challenge. I asked again and yet again. I continued to watch as I headed up the freeway. Strong doubts came. Why would I request such a dumb thing? Still I kept watching, hoping, and wanting to see if God would do that for me. In a few minutes, I realized the cloud seemed to have moved. The freeway hadn't changed direction—the road was arrow straight. I began to praise Him; yes, the cloud had moved! As I drove on and continued to praise, that little cloud passed right over the highway and was sitting on my left. Oh, what joy filled my heart! Almost immediately, I heard an accusing voice in my mind. *The wind blew it over there*, it taunted. I was so incensed I immediately said, "If that is so, then go back to where you came from, little cloud." I watched in awe as, very quickly, the cloud seemed like a soldier on assignment and returned to its former place.

I had no idea at that time that I would need that experience for the rest of my life. God would teach me small lessons so that I could handle bigger challenges when they came. I would face things much harder than moving clouds, but boldness to trust my Father in many different circumstances was growing in my heart.

I soon had an opportunity to again trust the Lord in this area. Once more, I was on my way to Canada, but this time it was late fall. Now the highway was wet and slick; the clouds were dark gray and ominous, with fog moving in fast. It wasn't that unusual to have rain and fog this time of year, but I had a serious problem. My mind went to the airport in Vancouver. My friend, Helen, was flying in from England. She was to accompany me to some meetings and also help with ministry. If the fog got worse, we'd be in real trouble. I began to pray for better weather; it was clearly not going to change unless God intervened.

I had no way to reach Helen—no cell phones in those days—and I wasn't even sure her plane had made it across the ocean to Canada. What was I to do? Again, I asked for wisdom and a weather change. By the time I arrived at the airport, I could barely see the parking lot; fog had taken over. Nothing was moving; all gates were quiet. Everything was canceled. I had nowhere to go and no way to tell Helen where I was if I left the airport. So I approached the problem the way I often did the hard things in my life: I decided it was time for a cup of coffee.

There was hardly anyone in the airport, so when a man and his very handicapped son came into the restaurant where I was, I noticed them immediately. We chatted a bit, and the dad said to me, "I need to make some phone calls. Would you mind letting my son sit by you for a while?" I agreed; his son posed no problem to me.

Once Mikey's dad was gone, I asked Mikey why they were there in such bad weather. With garbled speech, he said, "My mom is coming in from England, and we are waiting for her." I looked out the window and could not see anything but a blanket of fog. I asked Mike if he thought she could land here in Vancouver in weather like that. No, he said, he didn't think so. So I asked him if he would join me in prayer and ask God to remove the fog. Yes, he would.

I knew his mom must be on the same plane as my friend Helen, so we agreed we needed a miracle. Shortly after we prayed, Mikey's dad returned. As he took Mike to his table, I heard the little boy say, "That lady asked me to pray with her for a miracle so Mom could land." His dad glanced over at me and probably wondered if I had lost my mind.

Before I finished my coffee, the loudspeaker crackled on. A man whose voice showed his amazement announced that one plane—only one plane—had just touched down. It was an Air Canada flight arriving from London. We quickly went to the arrival area and had joyful reunions with Mikey's mom and my friend Helen.

Later, Helen told me about the arrival from the perspective of being inside the plane. As the plane flew over Calgary, she told me, a six-hundred-mile road trip away from the Canadian coast, the pilot announced to the passengers that the weather in Vancouver had been socked in all day. "We can land here in Calgary," he told them, "and bus you over to Vancouver, but I have enough fuel to take a trip over there and see if maybe we can get in." The entire planeload of people wanted him to try; that bus trip was easily eight hours in transit and wasn't anyone's first choice. Helen said, "I sure was praying for us to be able to land." She went on to say, "As we flew over the city of Vancouver, it was just fogged in tight, but as he circled the airport, a big hole opened in the sky. The pilot spoke again. 'I see a hole! Let's try to get in!' He quickly descended and landed so abruptly that hardly anyone even knew he had made it safely down. The pilot said it was like two giant hands pulled the clouds back just enough for us to get in."

I know for a fact that the clouds closed in again, and for three days, that fog shut down Vancouver International, as well as most of the city. We were able to inch our way to a motel near our speaking engagement and had fresh stories to share about God answering weather prayers. What a mighty God we serve!

> Ask, and it will be given to you;
> seek, and you will find;
> knock, and it will be opened to you.
>
> —MATTHEW 7:7 (NKJV)

39

My, Didn't It Rain?

PEOPLE OFTEN LAUGH when I tell them my experience of moving a little cloud, but over the years I have learned to let the word of God direct me in the many areas of weather prayers. I love Joanne Shelter's story. Jo is widely known as a Bible translator of a tribe of headhunters in the Philippines; she lived through many crises with her dear tribal friends over the decades it took to get the New Testament translation done. She tells of standing on a mountaintop and speaking to a storm that was bearing down on Balangao, Philippines. This particular time, when the rice crops were threatened, she felt led to cry out like Jesus did when He spoke to the storm on the Sea of Galilee. The typhoon changed course and the rice crop was spared.

Sharon made it a must-go to visit her family in Southeast Nebraska twice a year. This time, her parents' church invited me to join her and lead a mini-retreat for women in the area. We'd been hearing reports from Wyman, Sharon's dad, that Southeast Nebraska was burning up: The corn was stunted, and the soybeans were near a total loss. When almost all your income is tied up in two crops, the yields of which are tied into the weather, weather prayers get critical. We were praying about the lack of rain while we sat in lush, green, wet

Oregon, but it's different to be onsite, where you could daily watch the crops suffer from lack of moisture.

The day retreat was to be held in Nemaha, Sharon's hometown. A year earlier, Sharon had introduced the area churches to a George Otis film on transformation that showcased what could happen when as few as three people regularly meet for prayer to ask God to change their city. After viewing that, a local prayer meeting sprang up, with a good handful of people gathering to pray every other week. We joined their regular meeting a few evenings before our retreat, where the heartfelt cry was for rain.

That morning, the Lord gave me a scripture I felt was appropriate for our people; it was Deuteronomy 28:12a. The New Living Translation puts it this way: "The LORD will send rain at the proper time from his rich treasury in the heavens and will bless all the work you do." I related the verse to them, and we prayed. Then I encouraged the good farm people to just believe, because it was going to rain. Those dear ones had seen all kinds of weather challenges through the years and mostly lived by the verse that says it rains on the just and the unjust (Matt. 5:45c). They were polite to me as an outsider but were not convinced we would see rain as we closed the prayer meeting.

There's a story of a prayer meeting in India where people gathered in desperation to pray for rain. One little girl brought her umbrella, showing childlike faith that God would answer. No one else thought to bring one. As we left, I didn't think anyone was likely to reach for an umbrella! There was no rain in the forecast; practical experience meant there was more trust in the weatherman than the promises of God's Word. Hope grew, though, because everyone *wanted* it to be true.

Saturday morning, over breakfast, Wyman said with a smile, "It still hasn't started." Wyman woke up every day listening to the radio farm reports, and there was no talk of rain. I assured him it would rain soon. Almost immediately, it began to sprinkle. We started to rejoice, but then to everyone's alarm, Wyman and Donna remembered the community building where we were having our retreat had a very leaky roof. Several men had moved an expensive keyboard from the church for our special time, and no one wanted to see it ruined by the blessed rain. Quickly, we changed our prayers: "Father, could You please hold back the rain until after our meetings end?" The rain stopped immediately.

We had a great day of fellowship, music, and teaching. About thirty women came; two drove all the way from Omaha, eighty miles away. The hours flew by, and soon it was 3:00 p.m., time to wrap things up. At about 3:30 p.m., several men came to return the keyboard to the Nemaha church. It was a heavy keyboard, so it took at least two men to get it up the stairs and ready for the Sunday-morning service.

When we got back to Wyman and Donna's, Wyman had quite a story to tell us. Filled with awe, he reported that when they got the keyboard out of the truck, up the stairs, and into the sanctuary, *at that very moment*, the rain began. It wasn't sprinkles this time. It poured. The heavens opened up! It rained and rained all night.

At breakfast the next morning, I asked Wyman if they had enough. He smiled. "Why stop a good thing?" he responded. It rained all Saturday night and Sunday. On Monday morning, he said we could ask God to stop the rain. We asked, and it stopped.

Deuteronomy 28:4a, in the New King James Bible, says, "Blessed shall be the fruit of thy body, and the fruit of thy ground." The Father let it rain for two more days; the crops were saved, and Jesus was praised. I still marvel at the grace of God and His blessing to those dear, faithful farmers.

> Then I will give you rain in due season,
> and the land shall yield her increase.
>
> --LEVITICUS 26:4A

40

WILL THE FERRIES RUN TODAY?

IT WAS A blustery, stormy day as Sharon and I drove to the Tsawwassen Ferry Terminal to leave Vancouver Island. The terminal parking lot was packed, and we were concerned because the weather wasn't letting up. Hundreds of cars were waiting to cross the Straits of Juan de Fuca; all of us hunkered down in the storm of heavy wind and rain.

Finally, the ferry arrived and delivered the numerous cars that came from Canada's mainland. Just as we were ready to board, there came an announcement over the loudspeaker. "All ferries will be stopped for the time being. The winds are too high and dangerous. The next departure time is unknown." A dockworker had already told us that the last time there was a storm like this, boats were grounded for twenty-four hours. Other drivers started to turn around and head back toward Sidney and Victoria, but we were due in Vancouver in a few hours, so we decided to go into the terminal and grab a cup of coffee while we hoped for the best.

As we bowed our heads to walk against the driving rain, Sharon said, "Why don't you do your weather prayers?" It honestly hadn't entered my mind. Once inside and away from the wind, we prayed and asked Father to stop the strong winds and huge waves of this serious storm.

The cafeteria was bulging with hopeful folks who were also stranded and waiting. We found one empty table with room for four and quickly slid in with our hot cups. Just then, a young man in his late twenties came by and asked if he could share our table; we welcomed his company.

As we chatted with Colin, we learned he was on his way to Brazil. Apparently, he had met an attractive Buddhist girl who invited him to join her at a Buddhist retreat center there. Although he was raised Catholic in Ohio, he was still searching for something--he wasn't sure what--and was looking forward to learning more about Buddhist meditation. This ferry would take him to a plane to continue his spiritual search.

As we began to share our ideas of what or who could meet the needs of his empty heart, he listened closely. We took turns sharing while the other prayed silently for our fellow coffee drinker. At the end of our conversation, he still felt like he had to go to Brazil and find out for himself what Buddhism had to offer. Just as we finished sharing our testimonies and encouraging him to read the Bible, the loudspeaker crackled on. The man on speaker sounded surprised as he told us the winds had died down, and would we please hurry back to our cars, as the ferry was leaving immediately. The three of us stood to leave and we had a chance to tell Colin we had prayed for a change in the weather, and God had just answered our request. We didn't see his mind or direction change, but we did stand in awe at our precious Lord's love for that young seeker. The God of wind and sea used circumstances to give one person a chance to hear the truth.

Our trip across the straits was quite uneventful. There were no signs of the awful storm we faced earlier. We got to our loved ones on time, but what we experienced at that ferry terminal continued to remind us of our Lord's great love for those who seek Him. I hope you found Jesus, Colin.

Jesus answered, "I am the way, and the truth,
and the life.
No one comes to the Father except through Me."

—JOHN 14:6 (NIV)

EPILOGUE
INSPIRATIONAL BLESSINGS

PEOPLE WHO TRULY MADE A DIFFERENCE IN MY LIFE

First Corinthians 12 tells us we have all been given spiritual gifts from Father to help one another in the call He has placed on our lives. These are a few of the ones who come to mind who have been an eternal blessing to me and given me the courage to share blessings with others. My sincere apologies for important ones who did not come to mind in my eighty-fourth year!

Daddy John—my example of the Father heart of God.

Jim Bennett—his mercy often encouraged me. He was an example of steady love.

Grace and Don Kartevold—family overseers, faithful and true to getting all our family into the kingdom of God.

Lorrie Anderson and Joke Bergink—trustworthy friends, prayer partners, sold out to our Savior. Hardworking. Dedicated to the Lord's calling and to lives of genuine friendship and courage.

Fran Lance—showed me forgiveness, courage, and deep dedication in walking by faith as an orphan and lover of Jesus.

Jim and Laura DuPuis—took me in during my college days and showed me what a Christian home was like.

Chuck and Eily Chapman—made their home my home and taught me to pray for the world and encouraged me go there.

Linda Hines—my niece, a friend to many but she always makes me feel I am special to her. Very generous on all accounts, with a hunger for more of Jesus.

Gordon Patterson—shows me how to live with long-term suffering as he continues to walk with Jesus.

Mike and Lee Lucas—prayed, shared, and moved into our hearts as forever friends.

Howard and Janet Bradley—from my early days in ministry, these two and their family have been friends, mission adventurers, risk takers, and partners. No one has cared more for both Sharon and me. We have all grown in the Lord as we've walked this journey together. We love all your gang!

Bruce and Lorraine Friesen—encouraging friends and excellent examples of warriors in the battle for the Lord.

Dick and MaryAlice Timm—their home away from home and sacrificial love ministered to us over and over.

Chester and Shirley Royer—for the years we saw more of Chester than his wife did and for her consistent help with HOPE Center and our personal tax challenges—our love and thanks.

Kirstin Offutt—not giving up in really tough times; a loyal friend.

Lauretta Gray—always faithful, dependable, and trustworthy; she wears so well with people.

Clayton Potter—helper, caregiver, and a great guy to call a real friend.

Christoph Kind—dedicated and determined to be a faithful helper to multitudes, even with an aching heart.

Hannah Amit—prayer warrior, lover of Israel, dedicated to so many believers, always helping, going, giving, loving, and living a life of faith and intimacy with her Lord Jesus.

Bert Paschal—faithful friend, generous beyond words; eager to be there for us. Victorious in battles, loving Jesus, her real friend. Fun to be with.

Pam Morton—consistently generous and faithful, strong in her relationship with the Lord. Longtime friend.

Mike Morton—my dentist for over fifteen years, and I never saw a bill.

Dr. Dick and Mary Ann Cooke—now with Jesus, but long years of faithful friendship and an open home to us. Gratis eye exams for many years.

Olga "Toni" Nelson—full of the joy of the Lord, loving art, and inspiring many budding artists as she taught classes. They, in turn, were introduced to her wonderful Lord. In her nineties, she still sent checks for us to forward wherever we saw spiritual needs. A dear and special friend.

Ruthie Jordan—she always seems content, full of joy and prayer for others. She challenges me to walk without self-pity. Even in her blindness, her regular comment is, "I'm fine, I have no pains, I am grateful to be alive." We love you, Ruthie!

Viola Inman—always positive, a gracious friend and helper to Ruthie. I am challenged by her grace and mercy.

Larry Eddings—even in his old age, he continues to go forward for Jesus. He walks in God's faithfulness with a heart after his dear Lord. He encourages me to continue in the "Way."

Larue Rose—a giver of her inheritance. Her promise to Father: "If you keep me well, I'll use my money for Your kingdom, not hospital bills." She's been faithful, and that challenges me to be the same.

John Briggs—he came to Grace Assisted to retire, but we found him to be an incredible blessing, a pray-er, and giver to the kingdom. Oh, thank you, John, for your consistent walk close to Father. You love the Word and know it well.

Emil and Marla Antoine—the first to love on us when we attended Reflections Church; they continue to show us what faithfulness looks like. Thanks for being great friends.

More Inspirational Blessings, some of whom are in heaven:

Cliff and Jackie Bursch
Lilly Gross

Bryan and Lynn Yager
Adele Yager
Helen Guttery
Marshall and Loy Hickman
Pen and Joanne Hauge
Sue Halstead
Valerie and George Hires
Anita Hutchins
Blaine and Marge Highfield
Scarlett Kanistanaux
Garry and Melanie Lech
Gladys Lloyd
Terry and Carole Madison
Wes and Carol Marchbanks
Rowena and Barry McKnight
Neil and Margaret Robinson
Alex and Debra Paul
Jay and Meridel Rawlings
Joanne Shetler
Norah Scott
Heather Scott
John and Elizabeth Taylor
Paul and Florence Turnidge
Jeff and Julie Voudrie
Jean Wahlstrom and Marvin Kananen
Ernie and Alice Wiens
John and Lynn Wiens

ABOUT THE AUTHOR

Armed with a bachelor's degree in physical education and a background in both art and the Bible, Esther Bennett was a schoolteacher until, at age forty, she decided to answer God's call to the mission field. Stepping out in faith, she has trusted God alone to provide the necessary financial resources and direction for her life since the 1970s. God has taken her to thirty countries, from Asia to Africa to Europe to North and Central America.

Bennett lives in Meridian, Idaho, with her longtime ministry partner and coauthor, Sharon Pryor.

Made in the USA
Columbia, SC
20 August 2021

43364182R00107